Light through the Curtain

Light through the Curtain

SELECTED AND COMPILED BY
PHILIP WALTERS & JANE BALENGARTH

A LION PAPERBACK

Published by
Lion Publishing plc
Icknield Way, Tring, Herts, England
ISBN 0 85648 784 4
Lion Publishing Corporation
10885 Textile Road, Belleville, Michigan 48111, USA
ISBN 0 85648 784 4
Albatross Books
PO Box 320, Sutherland, NSW 2232, Australia
ISBN 0 86760 613 4

First edition 1985

Acknowledgements
The photographs in this book belong to Keston College, with the exception of those
used by permission of the following:
Aid to Russian Christians, pages 105, 125, 138
Camera Press, page 41
Derek Davis, pages 17, 85, 136, 157
Steve Turner, pages 92, 104

We are grateful to the following for permission to use translations which have
previously been published, or are soon to be published:
Chapters 10, 14, 21, 26 from *One Man's Witness* by
Anatoli Levitin, St Vladimir's Press;
Some of chapter 15, from *Our Daily Bread*, Burns and Oates;
Chapter 2 from *Mary Save Us*, Immaculata Press;
Chapters 1, 19, 42 from *Our Hope* by Fr Dmitrii Dudko, St Vladimir's Press.

Printed in Great Britain by
Cox and Wyman, Reading

FOREWORD

As coal crushed under rocks turns to diamond, so the Christian faith grows strong and bright under persecution. This was shown in the early days, under the Roman Empire. It is shown too in many parts of the world today where Christians are disadvantaged or persecuted. These include the Soviet Union and most of the Communist countries of Eastern Europe. One of the claims of the ruling atheist ideology in these countries is that religion will wither away as socialism is achieved. But since religion shows no sign of withering of its own accord, it must be encouraged to do so. Thus compulsory atheist education is used, and religious believers are often treated as second-class citizens, even imprisoned and offered violence.

None of it works. It is completely counter-productive. Churches are growing in these countries. Christian faith conquers all adversity, and individual Christians inspire others to follow them. They inspire us, too, as we read their stories. In this book we are bringing together stories of witness and faith from the Soviet Union, Poland, Czechoslovakia and Romania. They involve all kinds of Christians – Orthodox, Roman Catholics, Protestants, Evangelicals.

What should we do about these Christians? We can send direct material aid to believers and their families, and individuals or groups of people in the West can bring much comfort to them by writing cards and letters. A fundamental need, however, is that people everywhere should become as fully informed as possible about the true situation for religious believers in the countries of Eastern Europe.

The only centre for research and information on this subject in the English-speaking world is Keston College, which has a unique archive of Christian writing from Eastern Europe. Keston publishes a journal, *Religion in Communist Lands*, a newsletter, *The Right to Believe*, and the *Keston News Service*, as well as books and pamphlets. This book was compiled using resources and information from Keston College.

Philip Walters
Keston College, Heathfield Road, Keston, Kent, BR2 6BA

CONTENTS

The Countries of Eastern Europe

Leningrad

Gorki •

• Moscow

• Kiev

Odesa

CASPIAN SEA

BLACK SEA

Istanbul

PART ONE

CHILDREN OF THE LIGHT

Children and young people

FATHER DMITRI'S DISCUSSION SERMONS

'I'd like to say a word to you.

'A lot of people who come to church don't understand the service, the prayers, or the scriptures . . . People often come asking me to explain something they don't understand fully. Unfortunately, there are still superstitions among the faithful. Our Christian ideas are mixed up with non-Christian ones.

'Books on religion are hard to find. So, in order to meet the wishes of the faithful halfway, I've decided to initiate discussions concerning our faith.

Write to me about what you'd most like us to talk about, the questions you have, your doubts, the things that puzzle you . . . Maybe when you meet atheists they ask questions you can't answer. I know this happens a lot. All you've got to write down is the questions – don't write down your names.

'I think these discussions will be interesting for everyone . .'

And Father Dmitri Dudko was right. The discussions were interesting – and everyone came! The little Orthodox church of St Nicholas in Moscow was packed out when he preached on Saturday nights.

Father Dmitri's parishioners eagerly aired their problems on paper and their parish priest responded by answering their questions in his sermons. Already an effective and much-loved preacher, capable of communicating easily with intellectual and ordinary, unsophisticated people, Fr Dmitri's new 'dialogue sermons' were an instant success. Many were published and circulated in *samizdat* form (unauthorized pamphlets, typed or handwritten).

Starved of religious discussion, believers and unbelievers flocked to hear him. Fr Dmitri never meant to flout the laws governing religious practice or provoke 'difficult' questions. But when questions about religious repression were asked he didn't prevaricate either.

Inevitably, government informers planted in the congregation were listening. Such an open Christian forum could not be tolerated by the state.

Father Dmitri was "ecclesiastically disciplined", and suspended. His congregation were furious. When he was banished to a parish fifty miles outside Moscow many Muscovites cheerfully travelled to hear him there!

But the KGB were determined to silence him. He was eventually arrested and kept in solitary confinement for six months, after which he confessed his "errors" and was released, a confused and shaken man.

His dialogue sermons still speak to us, however. They have been collected and published in the West. They give answers in contemporary language to contemporary problems. Their appeal is universal. Christians everywhere, of all denominatios, can only benefit from reading them.

The following letter was read by Fr Dmitri during one of his sermons. He often invited young people to write and tell him of their experience in the faith. He used this letter to teach his congregation that life's bitterest experiences can bring us to God. Fr Dmitri did not endear himself to the communist authorities when he openly spoke of prisoners' experiences. But to expound on those prisoners' conversion to Christianity while they were actually in gaol was unforgivable!

« He Exists »

Dear Father Dmitri,

You asked your young parishioners to describe their path to faith. So I'm writing to you about myself.

The people in my family are deeply atheistic by disposition. Even my grandmother and grandfather were non-believers. From childhood I learned my lesson well that God is just a fable invented by ignorant people . . .

The more I thought about what lay around me, the more clearly I saw and understood that everything is gibberish, not worth a brass farthing. So I came to the point of rejecting everything and everyone. Concepts such as conscience, truth and morality were empty to me . . .

Nothing made me really happy. Nothing was pleasant. I started to drink. You get drunk and things get a little easier. The longer it went on, the longer it took me to get really smashed. On my days off I'd drink myself unconscious.

I got away with everything for a while, but you always reach the end of your rope. It all came very simply and very quickly. I got drunk, got into a fight, and found myself in gaol.

There was this guy in my cell, a Baptist who prayed a lot and would always cross himself before meals. Many people – including me – mocked him for this. Out of boredom I dragged him into a dispute over religion. At first, I just let my words run away with me, interspersing facetious comments about how old women just thought God up. He answered every one of my flippant arguments seriously. His unshakable conviction that he was correct began to irritate me. Soon – just for the fun of it – I began defending atheism seriously, proving by whatever means necessary that God could not exist.

I really couldn't have cared less either about God or atheism. I just wanted to break his confidence – that was the main thing. Arrogance pushed me on. And I achieved what I wanted. My cell-mate stopped talking. He fell silent, and then began to cry. He began praying that his faith would be strengthened.

I felt no satisfaction in my victory. A horrible weight fell upon me. I felt sick, like I'd done something mean to someone. And he just kept on praying, but more calmly now. Suddenly he looked at me and smiled. I was amazed at his face – there was something joyful about it, pure, like it had been washed. The weight immediately fell from my soul. I understood that he had forgiven me. And then a light of some sort penetrated me, and I understood that God exists. It wasn't even so much that I understood, but that I sensed it with my whole being. He exists! He alone has always been and will always be. He is everywhere. He is our Father! We are his children, brothers one to another. I forgot that I was in prison and felt only one thing – a great joy and thankfulness to the Lord who revealed himself to me, who am unworthy.

After this a strange and radiant thing happened to me. As a non-believer, I had read the Bible but had always hit on the "dark and incomprehensible". For me, the scriptures were "woven of contradictions". After I came to believe, each word of the Gospel was filled with meaning for me, close to my mind and heart.

It is small wonder that Father Dmitri drew such large, enthusiastic congregations. Completely en rapport with his listeners, he could gauge their mood, judge their response. A born communicator with a perfect sense of timing, he could refresh his hearers by introducing a little light relief with a few anecdotes. Nonetheless the anecdotes were always relevant to the main theme – the drawing of souls to God.

After a particularly weighty discussion sermon Fr Dmitri continues:

'I've probably worn you out turning over all these questions. For a little breather I'll tell you how some children once spoke about religion.

'Three-year-old girl: "Mama, is it true that everything's got a root? And is man's root his Soul?"'

'Seven-year-old boy: "In school the teacher was trying to prove there's no God, 'Because the cosmonauts didn't see him,' she said. But some boy answered, 'They just flew too low'."'

'A seven-year-old boy enters school, and his teacher asks: "Have you seen God?" "God is invisible," answers the boy. "You can't see him . . ."'

'"Papa, how come there's no cross on this church?" "Evil people took it off," was his father's reply. So the boy took a piece of chalk and drew a cross on the wall of the church . . .

'Two men stand arguing about anti-religious topics. They look around and see next to them a little child building a church out of snow . . .

'Let's listen to these children's voices and contemplate them. They contain a certain spontaneous wisdom and indictment of the brilliant, vain sophistication of adults. Indeed, by the mouths of children is truth spoken. A pure spiritual instinct draws children to God. And often in this way they expose our godless deeds.'

FOUR LITHUANIAN GIRLS

"Small is beautiful" is a cliche these days. Yet it perfectly describes the tiny prayerbook smuggled out of a Siberian prison in 1953. Small it certainly is – only two inches by three – and beautiful in its simplicity.

It was written by four young Lithuanian girls imprisoned thousands of miles away from their home, in extremely harsh conditions.

Perhaps no other country in the Eastern bloc is possessed of such religious fervour as Lithuania. To be a staunch Roman Catholic is indivisible from being a true patriot.

Like thousands of Lithuanians persecuted before them, the four girls who wrote this prayerbook turned to their one great source of consolation – Jesus Christ.

In their labour camp they recorded thirty-three prayers on little scraps of waste paper. Their pent-up religious feeling, their despair, their unselfish concern for others, even at times a little joy – it's all there on the tiny pages. These scraps were then carefully stitched and bound together. The little book, secretly smuggled out of prison camp, eventually found its way back to Lithuania.

Now, years later, thousands of copies have gone all over the world. The thirty-three prayers within are treasured for their direct simplicity of expression. They are proof that no matter how the body suffers the spirit can remain strong and close to God. Above all, the book reminds us that a crusade of prayer is certainly taking place inside prison camps in the Soviet Union – a crusade we may share by using some of these moving prayers ourselves.

Prayer can be simply described as speaking to God. If you possess no book of formal prayers, you can still talk with God as you would to a dear friend. This is exactly what prisoners in Russian labour camps and prisons have to do.

Surely no one has done it to more effect than Adele, Lione, Vale and Levute.

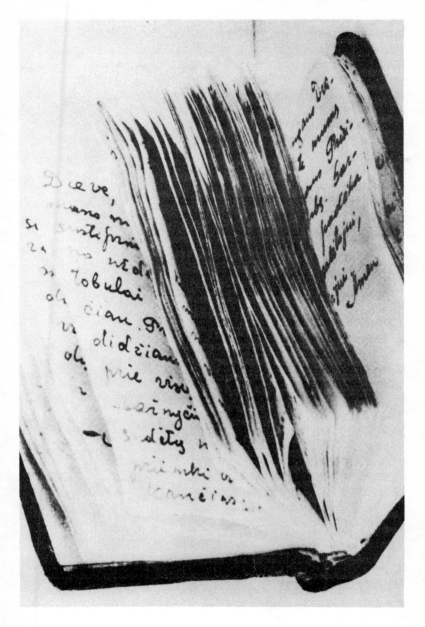

This tiny collection of prayers, measuring only two inches by three, was written in a Siberian prison camp on scraps of waste paper.

« Small is Beautiful »

O Lord, bless my sleep
The day has closed its eyes.
Fatigue closes my eyes.
My feelings have dried up,
my strength has left me.
O Lord, I thank you
for all your graces of today:
for health, strength, and food,
both that of soul and of body:
for every good word,
for every pleasant thing:
for hope, for my native tongue
that I hear
in this strange country.
I thank you for the suffering,
hatred, and all shortcomings
whereby you tested me.
Lord, I beg of you
peaceful rest for myself
and my dear ones.   Amen.

Holy family
Protect and foster
the peace of our home,
and our yearning
for the truth: shield from evil
the edifice of our nation,
and let us,
the children of sorrow,
spend some time
with our dear ones
in the fatherland,
at least in our dreams.   Amen.

I am in need
I am in need of a physician.
I am in need of a consoler.
I am in need of a Father,
the best of all fathers.
Jesus, my Lord,
you have remained with us
through all the days
in the sacrament of love.
You call,
you appeal to all
who are saddened
and weary at heart.
Longing, I yearn,
yearning, I desire
to be united with you
in the sacrament of love.
Jesus, my Lord,
come to me,
comfort me, console me.
Visit the hearts
in strange lands
yearning for you.
Visit the dying and those
who have died without you.
Jesus my Lord,
visit also those
who persecute you.
Lord Jesus, you are my light
in the darkness.
You are my warmth
in the cold.
You are my happiness
in sorrow.
The sun at daytime calls me
to come to you.
The twinkling stars at
midnight
beckon me to fly to you.
Snow and white blossoms
speak to me of your purity,
O Lord. Amen.

Pentecost prayer
Waiting
for the promised Paraclete,
the apostles prayed ardently
together with Jesus' mother.
Then came the Pentecost day.
Flames of fire
descended upon them,
enlightening
and bringing them
apostolic fervour,
the courage of martyrs,
wisdom,
and the gift of tongues.
Come, Holy Spirit,
Comforter and Confirmer,
come down upon us.
We are waiting for you:
we are asking for you:
we are praying for you.
Come and renew us,
come and revive our nation.
Bring us
all the graces we need
that, united in love,
we may establish
God's kingdom
in our fatherland.   Amen.

Christmas prayer
With icy lips,
with tearful cries,
tormented by despair, we fly
to your straw-covered crib,
O holy babe!
Accept our petitions
and prayers,
accept our longing
and resolves.
Accept the sacrifices of heroes.

Accept the tears
of our loved ones,
their sighs and cares,
steeped in sorrow.
Preserve us all
for a dawning future.
Grant heavenly bliss
to those who have died
in foreign lands
from hunger and hardship.
Through the merits
of your holy mother
and of all the saints,
have pity on my dear ones
and on my whole nation.
With a bruised heart,
I implore you –
cut short the days of our trials.
If you wish a sacrifice,
take it from me,
but give me
the courage and fortitude
of martyrs.   Amen.

Bless this day of toil
A day of hard toil is dawning.
Blessed Trinity, I wish
to glorify you
by patience and respect
for my fellow-workers.
Give us wisdom and strength
to endure calmly
all misunderstanding,
contempt, and hatred.
Bless those dear to me,
my whole nation, and
especially he defenders
of my fatherland, orphans,
and all those
who suffer for the truth.

Unite us all by lively faith,
unquenchable hope,
and love that knows no bounds.
Amen.

A LITHUANIAN EDUCATION

A small child's first day at school can be a traumatic experience for parents. Many a mother lingers at the school gate as her young hopeful takes his or her first steps to independence.

But in Lithuania, as in the rest of the Soviet Union, a Christian mother can experience real fear as her child starts formal education.

Children brought up as believers face problems from the moment they enter the classroom. Nurtured in a Christian home, they are then indoctrinated with atheism throughout their school career.

Every subject taught, from art to mathematics, is permeated with anti-religious propaganda. Directives on atheist teaching methods are issued to schools. Staff who fail to comply are frequently dismissed and debarred from further employment. Methods used in the classroom are bizarre: the tiniest children are encouraged to draw caricatures making fun of religion. Anti-religious posters adorn the walls, while instead of teaching nursery rhymes teachers may be heard exhorting their small charges to stand up and shout repeatedly, "There is no God!"

At senior level pressure is intensified. In the guidebook *Scientific and Atheistic Education in Schools* teachers are advised: "Senior students can be given assignments in which they have to calculate the unnecessary expense of maintaining churches and paying priests . . . It is essential that students be shown how this same money could be used to improve life for the working man."

In addition, all schools are required to run atheist clubs as an extra-curricular activity. In the playground non-Christian pupils are encouraged to torment and jeer at their Christian classmates – a crucifying experience for young adolescent believers.

Perhaps the most sinister feature of atheist education is the use of questionnaires and interrogation. Even very young children are held and questioned about their beliefs. Parents are not present at these interrogations when children may be intimidated and ordered not to attend church. Failure by parents to co-operate with the schools can lead to children being taken away from home. Certainly pupils who refuse to toe the atheist line – and many do – are victimized. Regardless of ability they are given low marks and poor reports. Because of this they may be refused higher education, and find employment difficult. As a state official lecturing in education once said, 'Once a child is born he is no longer yours.'

It is hard to assess the misery endured by young believers forced to live a dual spiritual life. Such children can become deeply disturbed.

While some parents are terrorized by the state, others cry "Enough!" When Leonas Sileikis was summoned for interrogation his father came along too. Such confrontations are commonplace in Lithuania, for despite constant pressure on believing parents, children are still brought up in the faith at home. Tangible evidence of their success can be seen attending churches throughout Lithuania every Sunday.

« A Parent Protests »

On 27 May 1974 Leonas Sileikis, a seventh-grade pupil at Siauliai Secondary School Number 5, was summoned for an interview with the head-teacher, at which his religious beliefs were to be discussed. The boy's father came to the interview, although he was not invited. The following teachers were present: Mrs Misiuniene, the deputy headmistress Mrs Jakimiene and five others.

Leonas Sileikis was first asked whether he had read the atheist books which the school had asked him to read. The schoolboy answered that he had read all six.

"What do you think of the books you read?"

Official atheist posters often hang on classroom walls in the Soviet Union. This one shows a spaceman who cannot find God in space. He is saying 'Boga nyet,' 'There is no god'.

"They are untrue and slanderous," the schoolboy replied.

After a series of attacks on religion, the teacher Misiuniene twice asked Leonas: "Do you now renounce your beliefs?"

"I have been a believer up till now and I shall always remain a believer."

After the schoolboy left the study, the teacher Misiuniene began to tell Leonas' father about the harm religion could do the children.

"It's not true that religion is harmful," Sileikis replied. "Nowadays religion is trampled underfoot: that's why children don't respect their teachers. They smoke, swear, drink, even sleep around – there you see the results of atheism."

"Nowadays only a minority go to church, so you should follow the majority," Mrs Jakimeiene explained.

"A corpse is carried away by the tide, but a living man swims against the current."

"You will bar your children from further education because of your religion," said Mrs Misiuniene, trying to persuade him.

"It is not I who bar them from further education, but you, the atheists. What's the use of science, after all, if you have to renounce the most precious thing in life – faith? It's you, respected teachers, who should be punished according to Soviet laws for persecuting children because of their religious beliefs."

"We will make your son an atheist in spite of you," said Mrs Misiuniene.

"I have been to a number of these meetings with you, and I am now certain of one thing – that you want to make him a hypocrite. You say 'believe as much as you like, but renounce God in our presence'."

FATHER CALCIU

The authorities at Bucharest Theological College were taking no chances. When staff member Fr Calciu began giving lectures on 'Atheism – A Philosophy of Despair', they locked the students up in their dormitories.

Even in cold print Fr Calciu's words still have dramatic impact. Delivered with his unique fire and enthusiasm they were irresistible.

In a country under one of the most oppressive regimes in the Eastern block religion appears to flourish. The Orthodox Church in Romania is one of the largest and most flourishing of its tradition in the world. Visitors from abroad see full and active churches. This suits the regime: the church is used as an arm of the state. The 'Department of Cults', backed by the *Securitate* (secret police), exercises rigid control over every aspect of church life from teaching to buildings.

No other priest in Romania has focussed more attention on the hypocrisy of church-state relations than Fr Calciu. Christian work is rendered ineffective by officials dedicated to minimizing church influence. Church leaders have compromised to such an extent that ordinary Christians are sickened by their leaders' cowardice. Other denominations – Catholic and Protestant – are viciously persecuted.

Any priest who openly challenges this situation is sacked.

Fifty year-old Fr Calciu was sacked by the college authorities in 1978. Not only did he rock the Orthodox boat, he also zealously taught young priests. Worst of all he was a member of the first-ever Romanian committee for religious rights, founded by Evangelicals but working on behalf of every denomination.

It was enough. He was arrested in March 1979 and sentenced to ten years' imprisonment on trumped up charges of 'fascism'.

Subjected to long interrogation, deprived of food and sleep, Fr Calciu denied charges that he had been a Fascist during the second world war – he was after all only thirteen at the time! But such treatment was nothing new. When a medical student under the Stalinist regime, he had been a prisoner for over sixteen years, three of them in the dreaded Pitesi

Prison, where an experimental regime had been designed to dehumanize the inmates. Fr Calciu was compelled to torture his fellow-prisoners. Among so much suffering, he realized his priestly vocation. Amid persecution, he was able to recognize the need for forgiveness. With his young friends dying around him, he offered his own life to God. After his release he was ordained.

Beaten, drugged unsuccessfully to extract 'confessions', confined to solitary darkness for a period and reduced almost to blindness, he is now a very sick man. He has been betrayed by his church — five of the hierarchy signed documents endorsing charges of fascism against him.

When his wife last visited him she found him with hands blue, bleeding and swollen — beaten by the guards, when they found him saying his prayers.

This piece is drawn from sermons to young people given at the chapel of the Romanian Orthodox Church Seminary, Bucharest, in March 1978.

« The Call »

The time has come, young man, for you to hear a voice which has been calling you. It's a voice you have never heard before — or perhaps you have heard it, but never understood or obeyed. It is Jesus' voice.

Don't be shocked, don't be amazed, and don't smile in disbelief, my young friend! The voice that calls is not that of a dead man — it is the voice of one who has risen from the dead. He doesn't shout after you from history, but calls from deep inside yourself.

What do you know of Christ? If all you know is what they taught you in classes dedicated to teaching you not to believe in God, then you have been deprived of a great truth — a truth which can set you free.

In your classes did you ever hear these words? 'Love your enemies, bless those who curse you, and pray for those who despitefully use you and persecute you.'

If you have never heard them, who prevented you – and by what right? Who stopped you from knowing that there is a better way than the one in which you now wander so blindly? Who has pulled the wool over your eyes so that you can't see the wonderful light of Jesus' love?

Friend, I have seen you out on the streets, young, handsome! Then suddenly you go beserk, lose all control; your face becomes distorted with rage. It is as if you were under a spell, consumed by violence.

But where did you learn such violence, young people? From whom? I have seen your mother – cowed, tearful. I have seen your father, his poor face stunned with pain. You certainly didn't learn it from them!

So where did you learn it?

Open your ears – listen to the call of Jesus. Listen to the call of his church. Stay outside the church and your violence will lead you to prison where your soul will be destroyed for ever.

I've seen you – standing anxiously before the magistrates, while the awful charges mount up. I've seen you – afraid, cynical, and full of bravado.

All of these attitudes show me how near you are to the edge of destruction. I ask myself once more. Who is to blame?

Come to the church. Only here will you find consolation and certainty. Only in the church will you hear Jesus saying gently to you, 'Son, all your sins are forgiven. You have suffered much. I have made you whole; go and sin no more.'

No man has ever said such words to you. Instead you have heard of class hatred, political hatred – always hatred. 'Love' is a strange word to you, but now the church shows you the better way – the way of love.

Up until now you have been ruled by your instincts, and your body has been a simple instrument through which your insticts expressed themselves. But now you hear Jesus pleading with you through his apostle Paul. Surely you know that you are God's temple and that God's Spirit lives in you.

You have been told that you descend from the apes, that you are just an animal to be trained. But now discover a fact – you are the temple of God; his Spirit lives in you. You are given back your proper place, your dignity as a spiritual being where God may be found.

We call you back to purity. If there is still one tiny scrap of childhood innocence left in you, you won't resist this call.

Come to Christ's church and understand what purity and love really are. You will be amazed to discover that life doesn't end in death, but in resurrection. Our existence centres on Christ, this world is not empty of meaning and value. You will receive hope. Your hope will make you strong. You will receive faith, and your faith will save you. You will receive love, and your love will make you good.

No man has taught you to fight your instincts; but Jesus calls you. Jesus is seeking you; Jesus has found you!

CARDINAL WYSZYNSKI

'It seemed quite natural to kneel and kiss his ring. You could almost feel his holiness. He had such authority and confi-dence.' So a young Polish woman describes her first encounter with Cardinal Wyszynski, Archbishop of Gniezno and Primate of Poland.

When he was appointed archbishop in 1949 he clearly understood the dangers facing him. The new socialist state, with its atheism and materialism, regarded the Catholic Church as the stronghold of superstition and the supporter of capitalism and feudalism.

Various methods, from atheist indoctrination to open persecution, were used to try to root out the church's influence in strongly Catholic Poland. But Cardinal Wyszynski was undeterred. He believed passionately that the deep-rooted Catholicism in every Pole is stronger than any other ideology.

Known as 'the uncrowned King of Poland', to the average Pole Cardinal Wyszynski *was* Poland. In defence of his people he was capable of implacable and courageous opposition to the demands of the state. While rejecting any form of violence, he engaged single-mindedly in the struggle for individual rights and human dignity.

Believing that the strength of the Polish church lay in the deep but simple faith of the peasants and workers, he went to them personally.

Catholic intellectuals were sometimes suspicious of his conservatism, and what they saw as his encouragement of the primitive traditions of Polish folklore. Nevertheless the Cardinal travelled tirelessly to remote areas of Poland where he attended festivals of faith, processions and pilgrimages to Marian shrines. He became a real father to his people: 'I am not a politician, I am the shepherd and bishop of your souls. My mission is to preach the word and to bear the light of Christ.'

The word 'struggle' figures largely in his letters and sermons. He saw it as his duty to put spiritual backbone into his people that they too might engage in the struggle between godless Marxism and Christianity. He always believed that Christianity was the one means whereby Poland could regain true freedom. Didactic in his approach, positive in his preaching, 'You will!' he proclaimed to his flock, rather than 'Will you?' And they responded – equally positively.

Subject to slander and humiliation by the communist authorities, Cardinal Wyszynski was at one point imprisoned for three years. On his release he said, 'Our heavenly Father told us never to retreat into the past, but to look to the future. So forward we go . . .'

His was the voice of Poland. That voice became silent on 29 May 1981. Just before he died he said: 'New times are coming which will require new luminaries, new strengths. I know that God will give these in His own good time.'

Perhaps it was his reward that he should die a victor, respected even by the Polish authorities, with a Polish pope at the Vatican and his flock united in Solidarity to struggle for a new Poland.

This address was given to Polish university students in April 1974.

« The Time Has Come »

Do not think that your identity card and your academic degree determine who you are. Who you are and whence you have come can only be told by the Spirit of God who is working in you.

The time has come to speak out fearlessly. For mankind becomes degraded and of less value if he does not respect himself, if he does not defend his human worth and his rights. The time has come in the confusion of our intellectual, moral, social and cultural life for you to raise your voices at last and to say courageously to your fellow students: 'Respect your dignity, for you are made by the hand of the heavenly Father!'

The time has come to say to each other: 'Friends, respect our girl-students for they are the future mothers of the new Poland. We want Poles to be born of pure mothers who keep themselves immaculate and by their behaviour command the respect of those around them.'

The time has come for you to say to your educators and professors: 'Teach us the truth and do not destroy us. Do not rob us of our faith. Do not destroy our Christian and moral way of life by a foolish secularism understood by nobody and for which so much money is spent. Do not deprive us of our faith in the living God. For you will make us into the slaves of idols.'

The time has come for you, young people in the universities and hostels, to dare to demand: 'Respect us! Respect each other! We are people. Do not snatch away our faith, for you cannot give us anything more valuable.'

The time has come for you to say even to your parents: 'If you cannot raise us as Christians, either because you do not understand it or because you have no time, at least do not undermine our courage to confess the faith. Do not make us sell our inheritance – the dignity that God has given us – for a mess of pottage.'

The greatest sin is not unbelief, which may be a personal accident or even human ignorance, but organized anti-faith, the setting up of atheistic programmes, the support of the atheistic system with administrative and public means. These means have not been entrusted to the state to destroy faith in God but to maintain law and order: not for destruction, but for construction.

The time has come to say courageously to us, priests and bishops: 'We do not like your indulgence in regard to laxity of morals. We do not accept that you have not the courage to require anything of us. If you discover faults in us, point them out to us – because that is what you are for!'

VALERI BARINOV

When Christian musician Valeri Barinov composed his rock opera *Trumpet Call*, there were no fanfares of publicity. There were no hit songs plugged on Soviet radio, and there were no reviews – for there was no performance.

In a country where even secular pop music is rationed, pop with a Christian message is banned.

When Valeri Barinov appealed to the Supreme Soviet for permission to perform his opera in public, he was refused. Worse still he was put under constant surveillance. Eventually he was arrested in Leningrad and admitted to a psychiatric unit where he was daily injected with Largactil – a powerful drug known to cause liver damage and drowsiness. When Valeri's wife demanded her husband's diagnosis she was told that he suffered from 'abnormal beliefs'.

There is no doubt that Valeri's rock evangelism was the reason for his arrest. A drop-out himself before he became a Christian, Valeri longed to bring Christ to the young drifters on the edge of Russian society. When he played the Leningrad clubs he always included a Christian song in his performance and carried an open Bible onto the stage.

Before his arrest, Valeri and his group secretly recorded *Trumpet Call*, in both English and Russian versions, on a forty-five minute cassette tape. Copies of this were then privately circulated among young people in Leningrad, and one was sent to the West. The music was broadcast back to the Soviet Union by a Western radio station.

The response was immediate. Valeri received many letters from young fans wanting to know more about the opera's Christian message. To young Russians any rock music has scarcity value, but Valeri's rock opera was a godsend in every sense of the word.

Now Valeri is working on another opera – 'Blind Bartimaeus'. Through his wife's persistence, and much prayer and publicity in the West, Valeri was released from hospital. Even so, he is declared 'unfit' to drive and finds regular employment hard to get. But his time is not wasted – Valeri continues his ministry to drug addicts and drop-outs in downtown Leningrad.

Sadly, Valeri's own Baptist church did not stand by him. Never at ease with his evangelistic style, the cautious congregation bowed to KGB pressure and expelled Valeri just when he needed them most. He has since been arrested for 'attempting to cross the Soviet border'.

But young Christians throughout Russia supported Valeri with their 'chain of prayer'. Parasite, renegade, drop-out, 'abnormal citizen'; the state knows Valeri Barinov only by these labels. But young rock fans in Russia know better. For them he is a musician with a vital message:

'Listen world, God speaks to you today.
Listen world, oh please don't turn away!'
(*Trumpet Call*)

These words from *Trumpet Call* were transcribed as accurately as possible from the English version of the tape. Some of the lyrics were inaudible and the transcription is therefore incomplete.

« The Trumpet Call »

'And he will send out his angels at the last trumpet call and he will gather his elect from the four winds, from one end of heaven to the other.' *Jesus in Matthew's Gospel.*

Hallelujah Chorus

Deo gratia

The gospel of the kingdom will be preached throughout the whole world as a testimony to all nations, and then the end will come.

This is the trumpet call which announces you about the second coming of our Lord Jesus Christ and about the end of the age.

Christ is coming! Christ is coming!
All through the years of hatred and strife,
Through tribulation, the troubles of life,
The good news of Jesus is with us right now,
Today and for ever – its growing power
Cry out, cry out, you holy trumpet.
Cry out, cry out with all your might.
Cry out, cry out you holy trumpet,
And warn the people of their plight.
Listen, you people.
Prepare for the glory of Christ.
Tell them the story.
Make sure that your hearts are right.
Right, right, right.
Closer and closer draws now the day.
People, he's coming
To tear down the way.
People, wake up now – you're all gone to sleep;
Prepare and make ready, you said it to me.
Cry out, cry out you holy trumpet.
Cry out, cry out with all your might.
Cry out, cry out you holy trumpet,
And warn the people of their plight.
Listen, you people,
Prepare for the glory of Christ.
Tell them the story.

Make sure that your hearts are right.
Right, right, right.
Hallelujah, come Lord Jesus!
Hallelujah, come Lord Jesus!
We are waiting you so long.
Cry out!!!
Closer and closer draws now the day.
People, he's coming to tear down the way.
People, wake up now – you're all gone to sleep;
Prepare and make ready,
You said it to me.
Cry out, cry out, you holy trumpet.
Cry out, cry out with all your might.
People are lost in the darkness of sin.
How much sorrow fills the earth.
How many tears are shed each day.
Who brought this evil into the world?
Man hates each other – where does it lead?
Why is there war? What is the need?
Who is guilty of this sin and shame?
Man, oh man, you're the one to blame.
This is because right from the start
You turned from God in your heart,
You denied that he's alive,
and then you killed him – Jesus Christ.
Where evil reigns, love grows cold,
Ah, ah, ah,
You lost your heart to the devil's soul.
Ah, ah, ah,
Filled with lies day by day.
Ah, ah, ah,
Can human beings live this way?
The world is filled with death and sin.
Ah, ah, ah,
The devil rules, he won't give in.
Ah, ah, ah,
Who is guilty of this sin and shame?
Man, oh man, you're the one to blame.
This is because right from the start

You turned from God in your heart.
You denied that he's alive,
And then you killed him – Jesus Christ.
Listen, world, God speaks to you today.
Listen, world, oh please don't turn away.
Listen, world, wake up, how can you sleep?
How can you sleep?
Listen, world, the prophecies are clear.
Yeah listen, world.
Yeah listen, world.
Yeah listen, world.
Brothers and sisters be ready, make sure that your lamps
    are light.
Christ is coming, go and meet him: in glory the bridegroom
    arrives.
Be joyful, nation of Christ. Be joyful, church his bride.
He is coming, our redeemer, to take us to God's right side,
Oh Lord, oh Lord come near.
We need you , Lord come near.
To you, oh Lord we pray.
We're waiting, come for us.
Still more time, yeah there's more time.
Still more room, yeah there's more room.
Still more time, time to repent.
Still more room, room to be saved.
Still more time, yeah there's more time.
Still more room, yeah there's more room.
Still more time, time to repent.
Still more room, room to be saved.
He is coming,
He is coming.
Listen you people, listen the world, he is coming.
Praise God – he is coming,
He is coming. Look at the judge, go out and meet him.
He is coming, he is coming, Hallelujah.
Come, Lord Jesus!
We are waiting you so long.
Hallelujah, come Lord Jesus. We are waiting you.
Praise God.

PART TWO

THE LIGHT KINDLED

Discovering faith

UNKNOWN CHRISTIANS

For every Russian Christian known by name to us in the West, there are countless unknown believers.

We hear of city-dwellers – articulate, educated –discovering sources of Christian teaching despite all attempts by the state to discourage them.

But what of the great numbers in the provinces, the thousands scattered across the farmlands and forests in remote areas of that vast land? They too seek a meaning to life. Maybe many collective farmworkers, villagers and small tradesfolk are ill-educated and inarticulate. Nevertheless they are shrewd. Their uncluttered minds appreciate that theirs is not the utopian life which their regime promises them, but that depravity and corruption thrive.

It is in this climate that unofficial religious groups flourish. The authorities really fear them. Not only is their influence widespread but they are almost impossible to trace and monitor, let alone control. What is more, employers are often shocked to find that the most reliable, hardworking and sober employees are the ones who are religious believers!

The majority of these groups call themselves Baptists or Pentecostals. They meet in each other's houses for prayer, but often take to the fields and forests where 'picnics' become occasions for prayer and praise. Frequently a riverside venue is chosen for worship where the rite of baptism by total immersion is practised.

This is a grassroots religion. Faith is sparked off by questions simply answered by evangelical Christians who have also questioned and helped each other to answers through prayer and Bible study.

Without benefit of profound philosophical teaching, great learning or ritual, these simple pilgrims set out to find their way to God. They may travel by different routes, but they reach journey's end just the same, armed only with courage, hope and the New Testament.

Here two of these unknown Christians tell their stories.

« A Dream of Healing »

This story is told by a woman who was brought up in a Russian Orthodox family and who had suffered all her life from the effects of injuries she received during the War.

One day I decided to confide in a brother from one of the unregistered churches. I sent a letter inviting him to come and visit me.

I told him who I was. Then, in great distress, I asked him 'Am I really lost? I can never find personal comfort in the word of God.'

He explained to me, reading from the Bible, that I could indeed receive God's peace. After being told, I cried out to God, and implored him to help me.

Then one day I had a dream.

In my dream I saw three men in military uniform. Two of them vanished – but the third took my hand. I peered closely at him. I could feel his hand firmly holding mine as he led me along. I glanced down at myself. All my clothes were muddy. We walked along the left side of the street, but it was absolutely necessary that we cross over. However, we were surrounded by very deep water – and not a bridge in sight. I don't know how, but somehow we found ourselves on the right side. I was so glad, so pleased, that when we parted I said to the man, 'Next time we meet I'll be wearing clean clothes.'

He smiled at me, obviously pleased.

Some time later, the brother visited me again, and I felt sure that the end of my suffering was in sight. The apostle James says, 'Confess your faults to one another . . .'. So I made a sincere confession to the brother. How hard I found such self-examination – as though the earth were opening under me! Oh yes, I had always said I believed in Jesus Christ, but I had lived without him. I prayed again, earnestly.

Afterwards I felt lighthearted, as if a heavy load had been lifted from my shoulders.

I told the brother that I very much wanted to be healed in body too. I asked God if he could perform this miracle in me.

But at that very moment the devil began to whisper to me fiercely that this man was a hypocrite, and that he wasn't really going to pray hard for me after I had made my confession. Men can't pardon everything – only God can do that.

I prayed again. And as I prayed I remembered that when I made my confession to that servant of the Lord, his eyes were full of tears. No! They were not the tears of a hypocrite, they were the tears of a man who was suffering with my own tormented spirit.

Before he arrived for the prayer of healing I just knew something wonderful would happen. I believed that the Lord would give me good health.

The servant of God came. He prayed for healing. When he laid hands on me I felt an extraordinary power pass through my whole body. I was completely transformed. Afterwards my depression turned into endless joy and gratitude to God for his all-forgiving love and mercy towards me.

We sang a psalm together, praising and thanking the Lord. It was not I but my soul that sang.

I had forgotten what it felt like to be healthy. After all I had been pretty well bed-ridden for thirty-four years. But now I want to run to the ends of the earth.

I want to tell everyone that Christ has healed me, body and soul!

« Are You a Baptist Too? »

I first became a believer in 1964. Before that I worked on a collective farm as a driver, a metalworker, and a garage manager. I was a Communist, and was considered a respectable man, even though I led a disordered and disreputable life: drinking bouts, bad language, beating my wife and children.

Many's the time I'd be staggering about the streets drunk and filthy. People would bring me home more dead than alive. The next day I'd start all over again with the wine and vodka. People thought that I was good company, and sensible too – because I was able to make money in various dishonest ways.

But I never took that money home. Instead, I squandered it on drink while my children went ragged and hungry. I would be away from home several nights running. In my fuddled thinking I couldn't even remember where I'd been. I had no idea of time, whether it was day or night. I lived in a complete daze. I sank deeper and deeper into drink, stealing, lying, picking fights. Yet in spite of this people in our village still had a good opinion of me, because this kind of behaviour was quite normal.

Sometimes, in the course of my work, I would meet believers. I would swear at them and threaten them. Sometimes I would force them to pick up glasses of wine and drink them.

My wife and I have a first cousin who is also a believer. We were visiting him in Kishinyov when he suggested we go to church with him. To me, a Communist, the idea was degrading. I told him so. All the same I agreed and went.

That church service affected me deeply. I could find no peace, because the word of God lit up the darkness of my soul. I was terribly disturbed. I blamed myself bitterly for having even agreed to attend. It was the apostle Paul's words in his letter to the Corinthians that especially upset me. They described me perfectly – fornicator, alcoholic, swindler and so on! I returned home utterly crushed, in deep despair.

When we got back from our holiday, my wife began to attend prayer meetings in the village. All that she learned she passed on to me. Meanwhile, I sat at home and did some serious thinking. I also read the Bible. Finally, I too decided to go to the prayer meetings. But the devil took care that some of his people should meet me. Just as my wife and I were leaving our house an acquaintance passed by. He was very sarcastic: 'What's this, have you signed up with the Baptists too? Look at this! A Communist turns Baptist!' It was not long after this that I became a believer.

The news shocked the whole village. The most avid drinker, most degenerate person in the place had made a complete turnabout!

The local authorities were especially alarmed. Thirteen of them, from the village, the region, and even the province, met to discuss my case. They offered me bribes: a car, and any position right up to chairman of the collective farm, if I would only give up my new-found faith.

All through this ordeal I sat quietly on the edge of my seat, and prayed. The Lord reminded me that he too had been tempted by the devil. All round me argument raged. They cajoled, they threatened, they lost their tempers with me. But I remained quiet and untroubled.

What more can I add? For I was spiritually dead and now I'm alive. I was lost and now I'm found.

ARCHBISHOP LUKA

On an April day in 1957 an old man climbed into a pulpit and preached a sermon. There is little doubt that his congregation was spellbound. For here was no ordinary cleric. This was the great Russian Archbishop Luka (Voino-Yasenetsky): monk, famous scientist and skilled surgeon. And it was his eightieth birthday.

The very idea of a scientist and scholar with a religious faith appeared utterly ridiculous to most people in the USSR. Yet for more than forty years under the Soviet regime Luka vigorously demonstrated his faith.

It was at the turn of the century that he decided to become a 'peasant' doctor. For fifteen years he worked tirelessly in his country practice, often performing as many as a thousand operations in a single year.

Then came the Revolution. In 1917 when he was chief surgeon at Tashkent he was dragged out twice to be shot, along with the others of the 'bourgeoisie'. He escaped death only because among his executioners were some former patients of his whom he had cured and treated kindly. Then his young wife, who had TB, died of cold and hunger. Heartbroken, Luka threw himself into his work: lecturing, writing, operating. He went without rest, and often without food, for he would not accept payment from his poor patients.

After Luka became a priest in 1921 he wore 'two hats'. We hear of him giving lectures on pathology, but always dressed in his cassock and always wearing a large cross – a practice which must have infuriated the authorities.

A priest is ordained in a church in Siberia. The Russian Orthodox Church has too few priests to care adequately for the millions of believers.

Bishop Luka was arrested and exiled – twice to Eastern Siberia, once to the shores of the Arctic Ocean. But wherever he went he began to heal the sick, and preach. If the churches were closed he would unlock them – illegally. We hear also of him operating on cancer patients, restoring sight – even saving a patient from kidney failure by giving him a kidney transplant from a calf!

Soldiers, fellow-prisoners, professors, peasants, fishermen, bishops – all have tales to tell of their encounters with Bishop Luka. These, together with his many letters, scientific papers and sermons reflect the charisma of a greatly gifted and holy man.

At all times he called on the faithful to be fearless in the face of anti-religious propaganda and persecution. He carried on this struggle until the day he died in 1961.

Apparently, even in old age Archbishop Luka remained tall and commanding. We are told that he still had a deep resonant voice, and the beautiful hands of a surgeon.

The words of his birthday sermon were recorded, and circulated unofficially in typewritten form.

« A Birthday Sermon »

I hope that what I'm going to say will not seem like self-praise. I must tell you that I don't seek my own glory but the glory of him who sent me.

. . . I know that many people can't understand how, having gained fame as a scientist and some reputation as a surgeon, I could then abandon surgery and science to become a preacher of Christ's gospel.

Those people who think that science and religion don't mix are terribly mistaken. It's just not true. We know from our history books that many great scientists, such as Newton, Pasteur and our own great physiologist Pavlov, were deeply religious men. There are many believers among our modern scientists too who have asked for my blessing.

. . . But I must tell you that I find God's work in me to be wonderful and beyond understanding. Now I can see clearly that from my earliest years the Lord was leading me to the priesthood.

Of course I didn't realize this. It never crossed my mind that I might become a priest. What I really loved was surgery. I was devoted to it. It completely satisfied my longing to serve the poor and the suffering, to relieve their needs by every means in my power.

I still remember with amazement something that happened sixty years ago. I finished High School and received my certificate of secondary education. My headmaster handed the certificate to me at the graduation ceremony – it was tucked into a New Testament.

I'd read the New Testament before. But now I read it again, this time from beginning to end. And I made notes of everything that made a strong impression on me.

Nothing made more impression than Jesus' words to his apostles at the sight of a ripening cornfield:

'The harvest is large, but there are few workers to gather it in. Pray to the owner of the harvest that he will send out workers to gather in . . .'

I was terribly shaken by these words. I cried out in my mind: 'What, Lord, do you really have few workers in your cornfield?'

I remembered those words all my life.

. . . Many years went by. I received the degree of Doctor of Medicine for my dissertation on 'Local Anaesthesia'. Afterwards I became a district council doctor, treating patients and workers – a job which gave me deep satisfaction.

As time went by I decided to write a much needed book on septic surgery. It was while I was writing the introduction that this strange thought struck me: 'When this book is finished it will bear the name of a bishop.' The thought wouldn't go away. But where did the idea come from? What did it mean? What bishop?

I had never even thought of becoming a priest, let alone a bishop! Yet only a few years later that strange persistent thought had become a reality. For by the time I finished my book I had become a bishop. There on the title page I wrote, 'Bishop Luka: Essays on Septic Surgery'.

It all happened quite unexpectedly – especially to me. Nevertheless, it was in response to the clear call of God.

I was in Tashkent at the time as senior doctor at the city hospital. When the diocesan council met in the cathedral, I also took part. I gave a long and fiery speech on a very important subject. At the end of the meeting Bishop Innokenti took my arm and led me outside. He spoke of the deep impression my speech had made on him. Suddenly, he stopped: 'Doctor, you should become a priest . . .'

I took this call to the priesthood from an archbishop as a call from God, and without another thought replied: 'All right, your Grace, I will.'

The next Sunday I was ordained as a deacon, and a week later I was ordained priest. I developed a great vocation for preaching, and also organized discussions separately from the church services. When atheists argued their case I gave them no mercy.

Just over two years later I became a bishop. It was then that the Lord led met to the distant town of Yeniseisk.

All the priests of this town, as well as those in the regional capital, were members of a church movement dedicated to supporting Soviet power. I therefore held services in my flat with the three priests who accompanied me.

One day, just as I was about to start a service, I saw an elderly monk standing by the front door. He stared at me, then looked as if he had been struck dumb – he even forgot to bow!

Eventually, he told me the reason for his surprise. Apparently the Orthodox believers of his town, not wanting to pray with their unfaithful priests, had chosen him and sent him south to be ordained by an Orthodox bishop. However, some inexplicable force compelled him to turn instead to Yeniseisk in the north where I was living.

Then I learned why he had been so dumbfounded at the sight of me. Ten years previously – while I was still living in central Russia – he had had a dream. He dreamt that an unknown bishop was ordaining him. Seeing me, he had recognized the bishop of his dream.

So it seems that ten years previously, when I was still only a hospital surgeon, I was already counted as an archbishop in the eyes of God.

You see how constantly over these ten years the Lord God led me to serve him as an archbishop during a difficult time for the church.

... I could tell you still more of the wonderful guidance of God's hand in my life, but I think I have said enough for you to cry out with me: 'Glory to our God for ever and ever. Amen.'

WLADYSLAW BUKOWINSKI

It takes a special kind of courage to survive concentration camp and exile. But deliberately to reject the opportunity to return home, in order to serve those left behind – this demands almost saintly qualities.

Yet Wladyslaw Bukowinski, a Polish priest, did just that.

He spent thirty-five years, including thirteen in prison, ministering to the scattered flock of Catholics in Soviet Russia.

His experiences as a wandering Polish priest in the USSR, without a church and without a licence to practice, are unique. Because of this, the Archbishop of Krakow – one Karol Wojtyla – urged him to write his memoirs. (That Archbishop is now Pope John Paul II.)

In Wladyslaw's memoirs we meet some of his 'parishioners'. Little cameos, often humorous, spotlight people such as Ivan the railway traveller, Dolorosa the sad one, and Audacia the formidable matron: when questioned by the authorities about Wladyslaw's priestly activities Audacia turned the tables, angrily wanting to know why the magistrates weren't dealing with hooligans rather than persecuting priests.

But perhaps this great-hearted priest was at his most revealing when he described his arrival in an old cart at a remote mountain village. There, against a backdrop of snow-capped mountains, he was greeted by a group of Poles completely cut off from the world. In their eyes he saw the tears of a forsaken people. He tells us how he felt: 'At that moment I felt intensely happy, and thanked God for having brought me to these poor people of such faith. I would not have exchanged the happiness I felt standing on that cart for all the privileges and pleasures of this world.'

Wladyslaw travelled miles in a hostile land to preach reconcilication to the Poles, Lithuanians, Germans and Ukrainians – believers and unbelievers. For him real peace meant the eradication of all hatred between individuals.

We are told that Wladyslaw wrote his memoirs 'in great haste'. Even so, not until 1979, five years after his death, did an unofficial publisher in Poland manage to bring out the little book.

Yet if we want to learn of the persecution and hardship of life under a totalitarian state it's no use looking to Wladyslaw for information. On the few occasions he describes his 'enemies' he does so with mercy, even affection. His only preoccupation was the battle for souls. After all, he might well be the only priest his people ever met, and that just once in their lifetime.

Not as single opportunity could be lost – not even on a tedious railway journey!

« What is Missing »

I was travelling by train from Karaganda to Alma-Ata. We were approaching our journey's end and only two of us were left in the compartment. My fellow-traveller was a likeable and educated young man, and we struck up a conversation.

Because we were speaking in private, without witnesses, we were able to talk freely. I even told him who I was!

My companion – let us call him Ivan – was Russian. He was a student at Alma-Ata University.

Ivan was a typical Soviet unbeliever: not from reasoned argument but because he had been unable to acquire any knowledge of religion at all. Seeing his interest in the subject I took advantage of the fact that we were alone. Briefly I explained as well as I could the idea of God. I went on to tell him about Jesus Christ, about his life, the sort of person he was. I spoke too of the fundamental truths of our faith. Of course if I'd said the same things to a Polish student, he would have told me that he knew all that already.

But Ivan didn't know.

Neither did he just listen passively to me; he asked questions. He kept on asking questions. It was obvious that he was very interested in what I was saying.

When the time came for us to part he said these words:

'What you have just told me is exactly what is missing in this land . . .' Those words came from the bottom of his heart.

ANATOLI LEVITIN

Volatile, voluble, explosive. Half-Jewish and proud of it! Thus Anatoli Levitin describes himself. One of his followers puts it differently: 'He is the very conscience and truth of Russia.'

A deeply committed Orthodox Christian, Levitin is a man with a crusade. He declares: 'I am a believing Christian. For me there is one thing greater than any other: the rights of man surpass all else.' Such conviction led him to play a leading role in the Action Group for Human Rights.

A prolific writer, he is known to Soviet readers of underground literature as A. Krasnov. His work ranges from controversial, challenging articles to profound devotional essays. Vivid narrative and a dry wit illuminate Levitin's work, but all his writing bears the hallmark of an active Christian love.

This love is most apparent in his concern for young people. A father-figure, he encouraged young city-dwellers in their search for faith by inviting them to his tiny flat in Moscow for discussions.

A young 'seeker' describes a typical meeting:

'Up to forty of us would cram into that little room. Amid a pungent smell of boiled potatoes and the all-pervading oil stove, a hubbub of young voices rings out.

'Tea is served in chipped glass tumblers, and lengthy discussions begin. Any topic may be aired without fear. Believers and unbelievers, Anatoli argues with them all, understanding and tolerant. He often says: "My flat is a corner of old Russia".'

But outside the new Russia waited. Everyone leaving that ramshackle little house was scrutinized by a woman standing outside – a KGB guard.

Inevitably Anatoli Levitin was arrested, questioned and imprisoned. We learn that his interrogators retired totally exhausted after their sessions with Anatoli – he talked back at them non-stop, hours on end!

Levitin is sixty-eight now. Following release after his third term of imprisonment he emigrated to Switzerland. He travels widely, a living link between the West and his beleaguered friends in the East. Presidents, world leaders, governments, Levitin petitions them all. The Pope found himself giving a completely unscheduled audience in St Peter's Square when Levitin rushed up and grabbed him by the arm. Hanging on to the papal sleeve he made an impassioned plea on behalf of persecuted Christians in Russia.

Onlookers reported that the Pope took Levitin's hand, and gave him a sympathetic hearing. He could do no other – for it was the very conscience and truth of Russia speaking.

These three brief stories are taken from many collected by Levitin about people coming to Christian faith.

« Found – A Faith! »

The young physicist
A few years ago, a simple elderly woman was approached by her neighbour. He had not long graduated. Now he was married and the father of a small child.

'I know that you are a believer,' he said. 'Can't you tell me about God? You see, as a graduate in physics I'm not satisfied with Marxism, and I should like to know the point of view of believers.'

'But I can't,' said the woman.

'Tell me what you can.'

The physicist and his neighbour had some discussions, and before long the woman introduced an acquaintance – a religious person better informed on theology than she. Gradually the conversations became more serious and went into matters in greater depth. After two months the young man turned to his wife and said: 'You know, after a great deal of soul-searching I have decided to be baptized.' To which his wife replied, 'But I was baptized a week ago, and our child too!'

The student

A few years ago a copy of the Gospels came into the hands of a young student. At the time he didn't read it. Indeed he quite forgot about it. However, a month later, feeling depressed, he opened it.

He was astonished, and read on without stopping. He found he could not accept it all at once; some parts of it he liked, but others he couldn't agree with. Then faith came unexpectedly as he read about the raising of Lazarus in John's Gospel. This passage, although a stumbling-block for many, became a source of inspiration to him.

'I suddenly understood how it really was, and I believed,' said the student.

That young man is now a doctor, and has become deeply religious. What is more, his wife, herself the daughter of unbelieving parents, has also found a deep and lasting faith.

The young writer

Eighteen months ago Yevgeni Kushev was baptized. From childhood this young man has shown a lively interest in social problems. He also enjoys literature, and himself writes rather good poems and stories.

When I gave him the Gospels, I was shocked by his reaction. Commenting on the Sermon on the Mount, he said, 'This is a splendidly written speech: it has the style of a publicity agent. All the slogans are properly emphasized.' This of the Beatitudes!

After that I didn't talk to him any more about religion. I felt it was useless.

Then, quite unexpectedly, he came back to the question of religion. He was going through a difficult time in his personal life when he suddenly said to me: 'I tried to pray. It worked. It made me feel better.'

Several months passed. They were very difficult months for Yevgeni. He was being persecuted. He was even sent to a psychiatric hospital for observation – where, incidentally he was found to be completely normal.

On coming out he said, 'I prayed all the time. I should like to be baptized as soon as possible.'

Today he is a believing Christian. Not once did he deny his faith, either when held by the KGB, or at his trial in 1967.

YEVGENI PUSHKOV

We have all asked ourselves at least once 'Why am I here? What is the point of my life?' But there can't be many of us who agonized over the answers like young Yevgeni Pushkov.

Yevgeni, a Russian music student, was born in 1941. He grew up to become, like many of his contemporaries, a seeker after truth. One of a young generation educated in atheism and materialism, he felt spiritually deprived and disillusioned.

As a music student Yevgeni was convinced he would find happiness in the music he loved so much. That happiness continued to elude him.

Then, quite simply, a few words from a loved one touched his heart and showed him the way – the way to God. For all his wide-ranging studies he found the answer where it had always been: in his childhood faith.

Diffidently at first, and then with urgent conviction, Yevgeni invites us to share his journey from scepticism to faith. That journey brought him spiritual happiness, even though it inevitably led to imprisonment for his beliefs.

A talented musician, Yevgeni learned to use his gift in the service of God, and thus found true happiness. He established choirs and led musical worship in the 'unofficial' Baptist church. He was especially loved by young people and helped with their religious education.

And all the time he was watched.

Perhaps nothing threatens the Soviet authorities more than church activity among young people. They believe that any religious teaching outside an 'officially registered' church building is a deliberate plot to wean people from Communism.

They came for him on a May day in 1980.

Yevgeni was working with a group of his young people when the KGB burst in and broke up the meeting in a particularly brutal and savage way.

Yevgeni was arrested and sentenced to three years in prison camp. He left behind his wife and seven children. In April 1983 he was released, only to be re-arrested one month later for refusing to 'register' his little congregation.

For Yevgeni knew that a 'registered' church can easily become a captive church, shackled to the state. He and his congregation need to be able to worship God, through music, when and how they want.

« Is This All? »

I would like to tell you about how I found happiness in the Lord Jesus Christ.

More than once I asked myself the question: 'What is the purpose of life in the end? What am I living for?'

One day I came across these words written by the great German composer, Wagner: 'Music cannot be an end in itself: music is only a means of expressing an end.' But what kind of elusive 'end' could this be? I had to ask myself, do I have a purpose in life? There was no answer – for I knew that I had none.

To find an answer to those questions which now tormented me, I became engrossed in science. Perhaps there I could discover real truth. But I found no comfort there. The only answer was most discouraging: 'Truth is the end to which humanity strives, but it is impossible to attain.'

I agonized over this: 'Can it really be that life is one long struggle towards a goal which it is impossible to reach anyway? Shall I, in the end, just vanish with all my aspirations, aims and hopes?'

Again and again I asked myself, 'How can I find out what the real truth is?' But not a living soul could ever give me a satisfactory answer. No one could say to me: 'I am the truth, I teach the truth.'

And then, I found it. Only one book in the world contained the answer to my question. That book was the Bible. There in the pages of John's Gospel I read those comforting words, the words of Jesus Christ himself:

'I am the way, the truth, and the life.'

When I was in my fourth year at the conservatory a fellow-student finished his course and received a diploma with distinction.

But on the evening of his graduation he left us all and went off alone to write a note. Then he jumped from a fourth-floor window.

The note was found in his pocket. On it were the despairing words, 'Is this all that I was promised?'

Not one of us could understand why such a talented young man, with such a brilliant career before him, would want to end his life so tragically. But nobody had been able to show him the best and true source of happiness. The world had cheated him. He had been quite unable to work out the meaning of life and had come to the conclusion that happiness simply doesn't exist. He thought happiness would just arrive automatically as he greedily absorbed beautiful operas and symphonies, but it just remained a mirage for him. Far from giving him satisfaction and peace of mind, the music only stimulated in him an insatiable appetite for something better.

My mother was a believer. I lost her when I was twelve. When I set off to begin my studies my father wept. He was a believer too. He wept over me a great deal at that time. He believed that I was seeking only worldly fame, and not God.

I remember one day very well. I was returning to college from my vacation. My father came to see me off. It was very early in the morning; the sun was just rising, the dawn just breaking. The train pulled in, and my father ran with me to the coach. Old and grey, he ran and wept.

'Why is he crying?' I asked myself as I climbed into the carriage. I found a seat and then, glancing out of the window,

I could see my father beckoning with his hands for me to come to the door. Just in time he managed to hand me a little note. As the train pulled away I began to read: 'My son, I weep for you. I thought I had sowed good seed but only tares have come up.'

I was deeply hurt. I thought my father would be proud that I was receiving an education. But it was just the opposite. He was weeping!

After this I began to think very seriously about my life – and about how I could know the Lord.

I decided, deep down, that one day I would become a believer. I also knew that I wanted to finish my music course at the conservatory. I knew very well that if I became a believer I would never receive my diploma. It is a fact of life here that it is virtually impossible for a believer to graduate from an institute of higher education. After all, how could Christians hope to pass examinations in scientific Communism and scientific atheism?

I eventually finished my course at the conservatory. I moved to Chelyabinsk, but first I was baptized in the Volga. I was twenty-six. I had to work as a musician for three years, but I was now a member of the church and I knew that it wouldn't please the Lord if I believed in him only in my inner heart while worshipping other gods. Music is beautiful in itself, but in our society things are so arranged that it is directly or indirectly in service to atheism. The greatest composers, such as Beethoven, Bach and Handel, are presented to us as complete unbelievers, which is quite untrue.

. . . A fierce struggle went on in my soul, but I couldn't bring myself to abandon my music. One day I asked my wife and my father to come to a concert. I was playing in it. Now, I thought, this time I'll saw on my violin for the last time and bury this music for ever. I will hear it in my heart, but I will no longer play on the stage. This music is not serving the purpose it ought to serve.

In the interval, I glanced at my wife and father. They were weeping. I don't remember how I managed to finish the symphony and go to them. I embraced my father: 'Dear Father, I hope you won't ever have to weep for me again. I'm giving up this music and I'm going to dedicate myself completely to Christ.' He embraced me too, kissed me; so did my wife. People were looking at us uncomprehendingly, but we took no notice of anyone. From that memorable day I consecrated myself completely to the service of God.

. . . I was too late to bring happiness to my own mother. But now I would like to say a few words to children of believing parents today. If you are not yet reconciled with Jesus, go to him now. Remember how many tears your parents shed for you. How impatiently they waited for you to turn to him. But you were deaf to the Lord's call; you were hardened to your parents' suffering.

But if it were only a matter of sorrow and parents' tears! By putting off the day of your conversion you are rejecting the love of God's Son who died for your happiness, nailed to a shameful cross. You are turning your back on this true happiness – but it really exists!

. . . Today, people who have found this happiness in a clear pure faith in the redemptive sacrifice of Christ go willingly to prison, even to death itself.

They lie down willingly on God's altar, if only to proclaim to others, and you, that happiness can be found. It is meant for you: it will be yours. You have only to reach out your hands today to Jesus, praying for repentance!

PART THREE

THE LIGHT BEYOND

Relationship with God

STARETS TAVRION

Beyond the state, detached from the ecclesiastical establishment, the 'starets' lives only to worship God. A starets is a holy man. Holy men have been known throughout Russian history, revered for their simple lifestyle and a deep spiritual insight amounting almost to clairvoyance.

Indifferent to worldly power and wealth, the starets is content to minister to the faithful wherever he finds himself – in prison camp, harvest field or monastery.

For centuries the startsy have cherished and guarded the essence of Russian Orthodoxy. Without their spiritual power the church at times might not have survived at all.

Even after the persecution following the Revolution in 1917, the startsy survived. With clergy liquidated under the Stalinist regime, the startsy went their secret way. Young people particularly flocked to them. The flame of faith was rekindled and passed on.

Today there are a number of startsy in the Soviet Union. Their influence is immeasurable. But because they shun publicity the authorities find it hard to keep track of them.

But people know where they are. Pilgrims will travel long distances to visit their starets in remote village, deep forest or secret convent.

Starets Tavrion was such a man.

He was only thirteen when he ran away to join a monastery – the Glinsk Hermitage. He was called up in 1918, but the Red Army soon realized that he was 'not of this world', and sent him back to the monastery!

In 1926 the Bishop of Perm made him an archimandrite. As he placed the mitre on Fr Tavrion's head the Bishop said: 'For the suffering you will have to endure.'

And the suffering came. When he was only thirty, Starets Tavrion began twenty-eight years of torment and hardship in prison and exile. A true starets, he continued his ministry wherever he happened to be – behind bars, or labouring in the great forests.

After his release he was made Abbot of the Glinsk Hermitage. Later he was moved from diocese to diocese. But so great were the crowds who came to hear him that he was banned from preaching by the church for fear of offending the authorities.

Finally he ended his ministry as spiritual father to a convent in Latvia.

Thousands of pilgrims – many from Russia – visited him there. Young people especially sought fellowship with other young believers on these pilgrimages. Such loving unity between individual Christians presents a solid body of belief which is a real threat to communist ideology.

The way of the starets is quiet, self-effacing, ascetic. Yet, living constantly in God's presence, his influence is strong. The faith is safe in his hands.

As Fr Tavrion instructed a young deacon: 'In our age the pastor must be at the same time an apostle, martyr, doctor of the church, theologian and saint.'

In this passage, a young follower recalls Starets Tavrion.

« The Way of the Starets »

Although the hermitage is in Latvia, in a silent, solemn pine forest, the place reminds one of an old corner of Russia, miraculously preserved.

'In the morning, very early, towards five, when the city is still asleep, there is such beauty here that we sing the Gloria and gather together at God's banquet,' explains the starets.

Nowhere have I seen services celebrated with such humanity, gentleness, and conviction – such Easter joy. Here one can really feel the strength of the starets' prayer, and the fire of the Holy Spirit.

At every service there is a sermon – often two or three. They are like a torrent of life-giving wisdom, not only baring the secrets of the conscience but bathing the heart with the great love of the heavenly Father.

What strikes one most is that it is not just the priest and choir singing: everyone joins in. Many youngsters from Moscow have learnt here for the first time how to sing the services correctly. The vigorous exhortation of the starets –'Come on, let's sing together, all of us!' – is unforgettable. Everyone responds . . .

His sermons are splendid – an evangelical judgement on 'contemporary reality'. They call on every Christian to repent. When, for the first time, I saw the starets preaching, his eyes closed, a Gospel in his hands, I felt that such humility and power could only be found in a saint. Many have felt the charismatic power of his preaching, and have found answers to their most difficult personal problems . . .

It is impossible in a few pages to give a real portrait of the starets. He himself asked us not to tell many things which we saw and heard. For instance, we must not recount the miracles which took place there, the examples of the miraculous insight of the starets, and his private ministry and involvement with individuals. We can't even tell of his spiritual life: we can only contemplate in silence his shining, luminous expression.

But I must speak of the feeling of absolute freedom which I gained from the first day I heard him preach on freedom. I could see it epitomized in the starets himself. For a year and a half detailed notes were taken of his teaching. We are convinced that these will provide a school of faith for many others. He appeals to responsibility, to vigilance, to a deep courageous faith – to freedom, repentance and holiness. We must be the salt of the earth. The hermitage and its starets are one of the most important phenomena in the life of the Russian Orthodox Church.

The Abbot said that in our day a true Christian would have to face death and crucifixion alone and that at the end of life he would not find glory and peace, but suffering and slander. 'But', he added, 'if you are crucified with Christ you are also glorified in him.'

He also taught we must spend each Sunday reverently, as if it were Easter or the Second Coming, urging us to unite ourselves with God. If we lack the courage, faith and love to attend a daily communion service we should at least attend every Sunday.

This teaching was underlined by his own illness and death. In November 1977 he developed stomach cancer, but despite this he continued to celebrate communion daily, though he could not take food, and was suffering terribly.

After Easter he took to his bed and never got up again. He could barely speak – no one knew how he endured the hours of his own lonely Calvary.

On Sunday 5 August, at five o'clock in the morning, the starets asked a young monk, Yevgeni, to give him communion and say the prayers for the dying. It was during these prayers that he died.

Three days later, those who loved him, particularly young people, came from all over Russia. His coffin was laid out in the winter church, while day and night they read the Gospel. Each one wanted to read at least a small section. Although the church was unbelievably crowded and it was difficult to breathe because of the many candles, yet a wonderful aroma came from the starets' body – there was no smell of death.

Like Easter, the day of the funeral was radiant, the sun shone brilliantly for the first time following two weeks of non-stop rain. When they carried his coffin out they saw the splendour of the sun and it seemed that this was not a funeral but Easter.

In the depths of light to which the starets was taken our souls sang, remembering the unforgettable image of his face.

AN UNKNOWN BAPTIST

We can only guess at the personalities of many of those whose writings find their way to us in the West. For obvious reasons some have to remain anonymous.

Yet if we read carefully between the lines, these nameless men and women take shape and come quite sharply into focus. In this way we may come alongside such writers, even identify with them.

Anyone who has experienced the anguish of homesickness must surely recognize the homesickness experienced by this unknown Baptist. His family, his friends, he remembers them all.

It is unlikely that he would have been steeped in the teaching of the mystics or those practised in prayer down the ages. Yet it seems he knew instinctively what to do. He poured himself out in a paean of praise and thanksgiving to God. Julian of Norwich, the desert fathers and many others prescribe this course when despair sets in. Our grandmothers put it in a simpler way. They urged us to 'count our blessings'.

In our blasé acceptance of Western freedom it would seem presumptuous to count blessings. We have so many. Prisoners of conscience have so few. Like this writer, who had just a tiny scrap of blue sky.

« Don't Close Off Heaven »

Prison again. My crime, 'holding a meeting in the open air'. In accordance with the law – three years' deprivation of liberty.

The door, without a handle, swings open and shuts behind me! It just looks like another patch on the dark walls. In the stuffy room, through the blue haze, I start making out the inhabitants on the two-tier plank beds which stand on the concrete floor.

The inmates are of different ages, and have committed various crimes. Nevertheless they are all equally rough and crude characters.

We get to know each other. I am cross-questioned.

I give them food out of my bag: they move over and offer me a place on the edge of an upper bunk. I creep up to this shelf, bent double, and lie down almost up against the roof.

The roof of the room is made of brick, low and heavy. It is dome-shaped – like an oven – so that noise echoes equally all over the room, creating an all-pervasive din. There are depressing grey stains on the walls and ceiling, and only two barred windows. Through these I can see a high fence, rows of barbed wire – and a patch of the blue heavens.

The heavens! They seem especially beautiful here, against this background of the drab colours of everyday existence.

This isn't the first time I've been in a room where I could just glimpse the sky, even if only through a little chink. But now the heavens have a special meaning for me. We hold meetings under the heavens, and my family and friends wander under them.

The heavens see everyone, and when I look at them I remember those who first experienced the joy of heaven.

Here in prison, amid foul language, anger and vile stories, I am deeply touched by God's great love: 'Lord, how hard you had to work on me so that I should come to know the joy of heaven. Lord, will you always be glad when you look at me? You led me out from among sinners and opened heaven to me by your suffering and crucifixion. Lord God, open it to others too. Lord, help me to be a true witness, and bring my fragile boat to safe harbour.'

Dear friends! What a great joy God has revealed for us through a saving, living faith! He is beyond price. We can delight in the radiant heavens. Heaven is beautiful every-where. Even here.

ANATOLI LEVITIN

With masterly understatement Anatoli Levitin tells us that condi-tions in his prison cell were 'very difficult'.

'The cell, only twenty square metres, was full of people: eighteen to twenty-six prisoners were billeted in it. The continual smoking, and the toilet bucket located in the room, poisoned the air. The inces-sant click of dominoes, the bellow-ing of the loudspeakers, created a deafening noise – a noise unbroken from six o'clock in the morning till ten o'clock at night.'

It would be hard to imagine a less propitious place for a retreat, let alone growth in the life of prayer. Yet Anatoli Levitin spent ten months in that environment and emerged, he assures us, stronger than when he went in.

He is a talented writer and a born communicator. Yet, denied these means of expression, he used his imaginative creative gifts to communicate with God in a way he could only describe as miraculous.

Archbishop Anthony (Bloom) once described prayer as 'a drawing of the soul into the very heart of God'. This was surely Levitin's experience. Oblivious of the squalor, filth and noise surrounding him, his inner self rose high. He used every opportunity to grow nearer to God.

On his release, he took up his pen and shared the whole experience. His experience teaches us that prayer is above the narrow confines of denomination, that it embraces not only God but all mankind.

« A Tired Man Finds New Strength »

I felt at ease and well in prison. I left it, strange as it may seem, with stronger nerves, although for the whole time I was subjected to very bad conditions.

I would be terribly ungrateful if I did not say to what I owed my feeling of well-being. I can say it in one word: prayer. The greatest miracle of all is prayer. I have only to turn my thoughts to God and I suddenly feel a strength bursting into me, into my soul, into my whole being. What is it? Psychotherapy? No, it's not psychotherapy. Where would I, an unimportant, tired old man, get this sort of strength – a strength which renews me, saves me, lifts me up above the earth? It comes from outside – nothing on earth can withstand it.

I am not a mystic by nature, nor am I prone to supernatural experiences. But I am susceptible to that which is available to everyone: prayer.

Since I grew up in the Orthodox church, my prayer pours out in Orthodox forms. My whole spiritual life is based on the Orthodox way of worship. So while I was in prison I 'attended' the Orthodox church service every day – in my imagination. At eight in the morning I would begin walking round my cell, repeating the familiar words to myself. At such moments I would feel myself inseparably at one with Christians the world over. So I always prayed for the pope and for the ecumenical patriarch, as well as for the leaders of my own church.

At the central point of the service I would feel as if I was actually standing before the Lord. I could sense almost physically his wounded, bleeding body. Then I would begin praying in my own words, remembering all those near to me, imprisoned and free, those still alive and those who had died. And my memory would keep suggesting more and more names – writers, dramatists, patriots, martyrs, bishops; and priests and teachers I had known over the years since my childhood.

The prison walls moved apart, and the whole universe, visible and invisible, became my home; the universe for which that wounded, pierced body offered itself as a sacrifice. All day after this service I felt great spiritual elation. I felt purified. It wasn't just my own prayer – it was much more the prayer of many faithful Christians helping me. I felt it continually working from a distance to lift me up as though on wings, giving me living watr and the bread of life, peace of soul, rest and love.

FATHER MALINSKI

Father Malinksi is Polish. Both monk and priest, he lives and works in Krakow. Ministering from his monastic order, he is mainly involved with intellectuals and young Polish families. A deeply spiritual man, with an unworldly air about him, he is very popular, and widely known through both his writings and his work in conducting spiritual retreats.

Cardinal Wojtyla, now Pope John Paul II, was a contemporary of Fr Malinski and they are very close friends. After Pope John Paul's election Fr Malinski wrote a fascinating book entitled *The Way to the Vatican*.

It is perhaps as a writer that Fr Malinski is most widely known. His column is published regularly in a Polish Catholic weekly paper, which is censored very heavily. Yet strangely Fr Malinski's pieces are very rarely censored. He writes articles

A Warsaw crowd awaits the arrival of Pope John Paul II. Millions of people greeted him on his two visits as pope. Poland is a deeply Catholic country.

with a spiritual content that give enormous uplift and encouragement to their readers.

Always topical to the situation in Poland, his writing exhibits a dry wit. His style is considered by some to be so subtle that the censors cannot read between the lines to see its deeper meaning.

Immensely readable, he understands modern Christians' difficulties. He gives pithy, practical advice to all who are trying to practise their faith in a hectic modern environment.

Some of these short pieces are from a book of meditations in diary form; others appeared in a Polish newspaper.

«Faith Day By Day»

Have Faith
Have faith. The faith that uproots trees, moves mountains, calms the sea, extinguishes fire, heals the sick, raises the dead.

Have faith. Live selflessly while others are trying to profit from everything. Be poor, while others are thinking only about increasing their wealth. Work, while others are neglecting their duties. Serve the people, while others are just wanting to be served. Be charitable, while others are thinking only about themselves. Stay in the shadow, while others are striving to glitter in the limelight. Have faith.

Be a light

Be a light. If the darkness increases around us, all the more reason to shine. Be the light of wisdom for those who lose their way. Be a light. The colder it is around us, the more reason for you to shine. Be a light for those who despair and are disheartened. Relative to God's gifts in you, even as a tiny candle or as a barely glowing light, but perhaps as a beacon or as a blazing bonfire, shine as much as you can.

A modern parable

From a distance you catch sight of people taking water out of the sea. You move closer and see that there are young and old, men and women. You look at their faces. They are red with effort. Suddenly you spot the containers with which they are removing the water. Horrified, you realize they are sieves!

'Father, you shouldn't be surprised that the children don't work at religious study: they've got a lot to do. When we went to school, there wasn't so much to learn. But my child's coping: all his marks are good – and that's the main thing.'

'Oh yes, it's very important.'

'I didn't go to church on Sunday. We went on a day-trip. The departure was fixed for seven. In the end though we didn't leave till eight, but how were we to know? We got back quite late.'

'I can't manage to say a prayer in the morning. I'm hardly up before work starts. And in the evening I'm too tired. I put my head on the pillow and I'm asleep straight away.'

The exhausted, the restless, the overworked – they too draw water with sieves.

A dose of appreciation

Everyone needs a daily dose of appreciation. People can't function normally without it. Children need it most, adults less, and the elderly more again.

It happens often that when a child is naughty, disobedient, spiteful, the best correction is for someone to take an interest in him, notice him, show him some compassion. When you suddenly find that your parents have become obstinate, impossible to get along with, that they are incapable of understanding anything, then give your father a smile, say a kind word to him, and give your Mum a kiss.

When you notice that your husband has got out of bed on the wrong side or that he has had a nightmare, say something nice to him, thank him for something – even if he did it a long time ago – and congratulate him on his achievements. When you notice that your wife is in one of her moods for no apparent reason, pay her a compliment, present her with a bouquet of flowers. And when you yourself are very tired, irritated, buy yourself a pair of warm slippers or some small thing. And when you cannot stand yourself any more, go to the hairdresser. Be able to smile at yourself.

All by yourself

When you pray, go into your room. Shut yourself in. Turn the wick in the lamp down. Sit comfortably. Lean your head back. Look at the Christmas tree, still glittering in the corner, and try to sing Christmas carols – all by yourself for Jesus.

Learn to celebrate alone. Learn to live alone. Don't leave everything to the crowd, the group, the society in which you live. They may be a help to you, but in the end you must act for yourself. No one else can make decisions for you. No one, however much he loves you. You alone have to do it.

Stay on your own. Start singing carols. Listen to your voice in the empty church of your room. You'll feel as you did the time you looked closely into the mirror and saw your reflection. Listen to yourself.

Learn to live alone. This is just as important as learning to live with others.

The fourth temptation

The first three temptations of Jesus were in the desert, at the beginning of his ministry. The fourth, before his passion, came from Peter's lips, urging him to save himself from death.

It is the hardest temptation. Different from being tempted to change stones into bread, different from being tempted to cast oneself from the top of the temple, or being tempted to bow before Satan.

It is a different thing to face death on a cross.

Maybe God will also ask you to die in defence of your dignity, your humanity, truth. Who knows? So many of your brothers have found themselves in similar circumstances. And they chose death.

It might not come to this for you, but you can be sure that there will be many situations in your life when you will have to pay for the truth with your career, with success, with your job . . . And perhaps a friend of yours will come to you and say: 'Don't act like a madman!'

If only you were then capable of giving the same answer as Jesus gave to Peter: 'Go away, Satan, for you don't understand what God's will is!'

FATHER CALCIU

'I speak to you about death – it's your only possibility of resurrection.' 'From now on, young man, be not afraid of death.'

'Christ is risen! From this moment on your life has meaning. It will not finish up between four sides of a coffin!'

When Father Calciu preached to young people he didn't mince words. He knew that they worried about death, and sometimes doubted whether there was life after death. He spoke with understanding to their inner anxiety and those fears that are common to us all.

The resurrection of Jesus Christ is the keystone of Christian belief. Father Calciu wastes no time. He takes us step by step through a simple clearly reasoned argument for the Christian belief in life beyond the grave.

Dag Hammarskjöld once remarked, 'In the last analysis, it is our conception of death which decides our answers to all the questions that life puts to us.'

How well Father Calciu understands our muddled thinking, our evasion of the whole uncomfortable idea of dying. Positively, yet sympathetically, he helps us to arrive at our own conception of death, based on God's love and promise of eternal life.

« You Will Not Die »

If there be no resurrection, if the only reality is death, then we are no better than stones. If we see things without faith, our life merely lasts from birth to death. We might live a day, or we could live for seventy years, for from the minute we are born we are old enough to die.

What sense is there then, in this short interval in face of the 'foreverness' of death? Are we simply here to fall like a stone loosened from its pile, or die like a calf butchered in the slaughterhouse? Such a death is inhuman. It is a nightmare, for beyond it there is no light, only a dreadful darkness.

. . . Yet Jesus has given us a death without fear. He assures us that death is not the end, but the beginning of eternal life through his resurrection.

To love someone is to say 'you will not die'. We really believe what we say. This blind, irrational belief is not open to argument. It is the only basic truth which we experience fully when we love others.

I am speaking of all kinds of love: the mother nursing her child says to him with a faith that moves mountains, 'You will not die'. She believes it. The beloved who buries a dear one, uttering words of passion to melt the coffin, is really saying, 'You will not die'. She believes it.

Man's dark history knew one moment of sunshine, which since then has been pouring out on humanity. I speak of the

Sun of Righteousness, Jesus Christ the Son of God who came into the world to save us. Why did God, who knew no need, feel compelled to become man? Only for love, for only love sets us free. This is not a passionate love, but a compassionate love.

... In this way Jesus Christ, crucified for us, became tangible love. It was hard for men to believe what they saw – perfect love in human form. They had to prove that love, test it to the limit, to see if it could endure to the end. Jesus passed that test.

... If you believe it when you tell your loved one, 'You will not die', why do you not believe Jesus when he promises you eternal life?

My friend, you know that you believe, and I know that you do too – even if what you believe is not very clear. But those who try to confine your young soul in narrow atheism fear your faith more than anything else. Ideas only flourish when they are true. An idea which has to be kept in place by force is inwardly false. If atheists don't speak of death it is because they are frightened of it ... And just as much as they are afraid of death, they are afraid of your spiritual freedom.

TRAIAN DORZ

Robert Graves once defined a good poem as one that makes sense, and says all it has to say memorably and economically.

Traian Dorz' poem 'Distance and Isolation' amply fulfils those requirements. It has a tranquil quality. Without sentimentality it distils the essence of the relief experienced by a mature Christian when he puts his hand into the hand of God.

Traian Dorz is well qualified to write about physical and spiritual isolation. He has spent at least a decade in prison.

Now aged seventy-two, he is well loved not only for his prolific output of Christian poetry but as a leader of 'The Lord's Army' – a lay Christian renewal group within the Romanian Orthodox church.

Traian was only sixteen when he joined 'The Lord's Army' in 1928. Very soon he was publishing his religious poetry and helping to edit the movement's publications. In 1948 the Communists banned the movement for its evangelistic activities and many leaders and members were imprisoned.

But Traian's writing did not cease. Even in prison he continued to write poems and hymns which were eventually typed and circulated secretly. 'The Lord's Army', forced to go underground, still continued its activities.

The Communist authorities continued their harassment also. After his release from prison, Traian was kept under house arrest in the mountains of Western Transylvania. Despite constant police searches and interrogation, he continued to write and campaign for the official recognition of 'The Lord's Army' movement. For this he was threatened with psychiatric treatment.

Sadly, he was rearrested in February 1982 following the discovery by police of Bibles and copies of his poems (printed in the West) in the car of two other Lord's Army members.

At 11a.m. on 3 August 1982 Traian Dorz was taken to the prison at Satu Mare to begin a two-year sentence (from which he was released after six months). When his daughter and granddaughter visited him they were allowed just twenty minutes. Traian's daughter reported that he seemed happy and content despite his situation.

We have only to read this poem to appreciate from whom he draws his quiet inner strength and contentment.

« Distance and Isolation »

Distance and isolation enclose me like a citadel
and often through the black horizon
no thought squeezes through to me;

but when I come to you, Lord,
all is easy and bright for me.
Desolations and pains burn and tear me
and on all four horizons I see only storms;
but when I come to you, Lord,
all is peaceful and bright for me.
Disquiet and threats surround me like a sea
and as far as I look into the distance
I see no road of escape;
but when I turn to you, Lord,
all is free and bright for me.

PART FOUR

THE LIGHT IN THE WORLD

Living in society

ZOYA KRAKHMALNIKOVA

In front of the gate he could see the tracks of the huge state security car which had been and gone. His daughter stood by the gate holding her baby son in her arms. Then she told him they had taken his wife away. He felt bitterly ashamed.

Writer Felix Svetov uses the word 'ashamed' repeatedly in his account of the nightmare endured by his family that night in August 1982. For Zoya, his wife, he has only pride and love. His shame is for Russia, where such persecution is possible.

He felt compelled to write his open letter to tell us of his wife's selfless work for her country and her church.

Zoya Krakhmalnikova is fifty-five. She is well known as the compiler of *Nadezhda*, a little journal of Christian writing. A gifted writer and intellectual, she has many publications to her credit. Like many of the literary intelligentsia in Moscow, Zoya and Felix gradually turned to Christianity. She became a member of the Russian Orthodox church in 1971. Realizing the dearth of religious publications in Russia, she compiled an occasional journal of spiritual writings in an attempt to preserve the Orthodox heritage for future generations.

Together in their Moscow flat, Felix and Zoya worked at their desks. Their papers, manuscripts, copies of *Nadezhda*, piled up. On the shelves lay their novels, articles, stories – years of literary effort.

Only hours before Zoya was arrested at their holiday cottage outside Moscow, Felix, his son and other friends all had their flats meticulously searched. Books, personal belongings, even baby clothes, all were rummaged through. Manuscripts of *Nadezhda*, Bibles and precious religious books were stuffed into canvas bags and confiscated.

In a country where there is a ban on all unofficial religious publishing such 'night operations' are not unusual. The state security cars with their captains, lieutenants and 'conscripted' witnesses arrive under cover of darkness. Writers and intellectuals must tailor their output, or take the consequences.

For Zoya, the consequences are grim. One year's imprisonment – affording no exercise. Five years' exile – particularly dangerous for a woman alone. Zoya will then have to seek permission to return to Moscow, so she is removed from circulation for most of the decade. And her health is already poor.

In a document sent to Christians in the West, friends write movingly: 'Up until now Zoya gave, and we took. Now the time has come for us to give . . . Let us pray for her. We ask you to pray for her too.'

Here Felix writes about Zoya and himself, and what their goal was in their writing.

« Nadezhda – a Book Called 'Hope' »

We are professional writers. Hundreds of our articles and seven books have been printed in Soviet editions. Like many of our contemporaries we followed the usual course of Russian writers in the fifties and sixties, being closely involved with literature in a period when 'thaws' and 'squeezes' were imposed on publications.

It was during this time that we came to the church, and to know God. There was nothing extraordinary about this, except that a miracle occurred. Christ was revealed to us!

Perhaps we were helped by the love and anguish we felt for our native country: perhaps we were fortunate in meeting people who helped us to see something previously hidden. Perhaps books appeared on our desks which revealed what we had failed to discover . . . Whatever the reason, Christ became real for us in no uncertain manner. We met him. We saw him – moving across our land.

This encounter was a turning-point for us both. We were full of strength and energy. We did not know why we had been given this gift, but we gladly shared it with our friends.

We were professional writers. We weren't idle. Yet perhaps we could have done more. I regret every day, every hour wasted. Even so we achieved a good deal: twenty books, novels, stories, in which the beginnings of the new literature were written – and all created in our own home.

Now comes the difficult part of my letter. It seems almost impossible to express adequately what I wish to say about myself and Zoya – the one so close to me. Yet I must try, for no one else will.

We are talking here about a 'new literature' – new, because in our time there has been no religious literature. But we didn't just invent something, make something up. We simply lived our new life as Orthodox Christians, and we found we were living in the tradition of Russian literature. Dostoyevsky was closest to us.

But our whole difficulty lay in the fact that this tradition had been destroyed and our links with it severed. We had first to rediscover those links, build across the yawning abyss and gain access to the tradition.

Oh yes, we were brash, over-enthusiastic converts, and we made mistakes. But we were full of courage, for we had a sincere faith in Christ. We were no longer alone, and we had our life in the church to support our efforts to bring our culture back into that church.

My wife took on little purely creative work at this time, for she realized the great need for Christian reading matter.

'For Christ's sake give us at least some book about God!' She couldn't refuse to respond to this cry, born of the spiritual hunger of thousands of fellow-countrymen starved of spiritual sustenance.

Thus was born the idea of *Nadezhda* ('Hope') – a series of books of Christian writing.

Traditional books like these have been published in Russia since the beginning of the last century. Good, spiritually valuable, they played their part in Christ's cause. But in those days they used to be published in a climate of Christian belief, when thousands of Orthodox churches and hundreds of monasteries and seminaries flourished.

When *Nadezhda* was published it was alone, in a vacuum – launched on a sea of atheism incapable of supporting anyone. But it was filled with our sad experience, the tragedy of our church. This immediately raised the level of these new books. . .

As a matter of principe, they are never political, and cannot be a commercial proposition.

A miscellany of writing, *Nadezhda* contains pastoral epistles, teaching of the holy fathers which are unavailable elsewhere, testimonies and sayings of our pious martyrs. Also included are letters from exiled bishops and priests and contemporary religious teaching. These amazing documents were written by people concerned not to write about themselves, but only to write of their beliefs in order to strengthen their followers in holiness and spiritual fortitude . . .

The compiler of *Nadezhda*, Zoya Krakhmalnikova, also contributed articles on the tragedy of a culture separated from the church, and on hope for that culture's return to the church.

Zoya, as compiler, worked alone. Her work was rendered even more difficult by our inability today to comprehend its true meaning. Our thinking has become so distanced from the church: we've become so conditioned by superficialities, sensation, politics, and modernism.

These books are written for posterity, they are before their time. Yet even today they are read avidly and copies are even distributed in manuscript form.

I know of many instances where *Nadezhda* has brought people into the church and to God. Now Christians have raised funds to publish it in the West. Six properly printed issues have been returned to us.

Throughout all the years of *Nadezhda's* existence – six to seven years – not once did the authorities warn Zoya that her work as compiler was illegal. She has not in fact broken the law; she lived and worked according to her Christian conscience.

Nadezhda is still giving spiritual comfort, it is still strengthening readers in their faith and bringing them into the church.

The deed is done! The rest is in the hands of the Lord.

DMITRI DUDKO AND ANONYMOUS PARISHIONERS

When Father Dmitri Dudko was banished to minister to the little parish of Grebnevo outside Moscow, he might have expected some respite from the KGB.

But his peace was shortlived. It was not long before the authorities began to put pressure on both priest and congregation. To be one of Father Dmitri's 'spiritual children' – as the many young followers surrounding him were called – was to court victimization. The authorities tried to persuade the Parish Council to remove Father Dmitri.

Bravely, they refused.

Retribution was swift. Father Dmitri's house-gate was locked and his letters were confiscated. His visitors and members of his congregation were constantly watched and identified in order to intimidate them. But perhaps the cruellest blow was the forcible psychiatric examination of Father Dmitri's seventeen-year-old son after he had been found wearing a baptismal cross. Many believed that this was a calculated move to intimidate his father.

Instead Father Dmitri went even further in his efforts to minister to his people by starting a parish newsletter, *In the Light of the Transfiguration*. In no way an academic magazine, the little publication answered parishioners' questions, offered spiritual advice, included devotional articles and members' personal stories. This was a courageous and novel innovation, for nowhere in the USSR are congregations allowed to publish newsletters or literature of any kind.

In this piece from one of Father Dmitri's newsletters, we read a personal account by a pensioner of the way she and many like her have to live the Christian life in the USSR today. Her story, told in her words, can tell us more about pressure on religious believers in the USSR than volumes of tightly packed prose. The overall tone of this little account is positive and happy. But there is no escaping the underlying fear that held the writer back from free Christian fellowship, or the feelings of guilt at failing to witness to her faith at her workplace.

Such unvarnished, sincere testimony is irresistible, as is Father Dmitri's typically encouraging editor's note!

Sadly the last issue of *In the Light of the Transfiguration* that we heard about in the West was No. 83, dated February 1981.

« Secret Christians »

It's strange how people nowadays can't wait for their pension; yet a pension is a sure sign that you've reached an advanced age! This has intrigued me for a long time, but all is now explained.

I was coming out of church with an elderly lady I'd been standing next to during the service. Formally, of course, we 'didn't know each other', but that didn't stop us feeling a warm spiritual kinship. I told her about my troubles at work: I'd been sacked. I think one of the reasons was that it's 'not right' for an ideological worker to go to church.

'Yes, that's true,' she agreed. Then she went on to tell me what had happened to her.

'For almost forty years I worked in a special closed factory, and I got to know a lot of other workers there. I was great friends with four women – and now I'm on my pension we're even closer. They're like family to me, and here's why: we always shared our joys and sorrows, helped and supported each other, we couldn't live without each other. I thought my friends had no secrets from me. But I had one secret which I kept well hidden.

'I told them about it the moment I started drawing my pension. I believe in God, and I'd been going to church all the forty years we'd been friends. Forgive me, my dear friends, I said, for not being open with you. It's this life we live which forced me to keep quiet. Lord, forgive my sinful soul!

'I had nothing more to fear, so I made the sign of the cross with a feeling of immense relief. Imagine my surprise when all four of my friends at once burst into tears, crossed themselves, and fell on their knees in front of the icon which, now I need not fear for my relatives, I keep with a lamp burning continually in front of it. Just like me, fearing nothing, rejoicing in their new freedom, they too prayed: "Lord, forgive my sinful soul!"

'Now we talk about the church quite freely; we ring each other up to arrange when we're going to church. Lord, how good it is to get old so that we can talk freely about God!'

Editor's comment: No, you've grown young again, not old. The youngest man would say this about *real* old age.

FATHER CALCIU

When Father Calciu announced his series of Lenten addresses for students, he called his talks 'Meditations'. No doubt he would have chosen the word Meditation carefully – as befitted a professor of language. Our dictionaries tell us that the word derives from the Greek *medomai* – to think about something, to exercise the mind. Fr Calciu appreciated that his young listeners had agile minds. He was, after all, preaching in a college chapel to the students.

But Fr Calciu is a practical man. He knew the problems and risks facing both his listeners and the church in Romania. He did not just throw out fine phrases laced with rhetorical questions. He posed real questions, and then gave practical answers.

On this occasion he tackled the question of freedom – or rather the lack of it.

He knew from his own bitter experience that once outside the chapel his young hearers would be forced to live out their faith under a regime completely opposed to individual

The spiritual roots of the Romanian Orthodox Church have in the past drawn sustenance from the monasteries. This is the Antim monastery, which until autumn 1984 held the offices of the church's Department of Foreign Relations. The monastery has since been partially demolished to make way for urban reconstruction.

religious freedom, and that the theological education provided by the church, tied as it is to the state's policies, is not designed to help students challenge this situation.

How to rediscover that freedom?

Skilfully, Fr Calciu shows the young Christians before him how to find it in a liberated church.

How to gain entry to that church?

Again Fr Calciu points the way – a way through doors that have always been open, and much closer to his young listeners than they may have realized.

As he once said: 'Let us build churches in our own enlightened hearts.'

« Finding Freedom »

Do you remember how I told you last time that a new voice is calling you – the voice of Jesus? But from where, and to what, does he call you? What tempting promise does he make to quench your thirst for knowledge and truth? He calls you to his church.

You live within a family, a society and a world. You are bonded to your family by inescapable blood-ties. Betray it, reject it, and your suffering will be its own vengeance. You live in the midst of a people which you feel to be not just a group of isolated individuals, but one huge, united soul with which your own existence is identified. Finally, you live in a world of suffering and joys to which you respond because something in you unites and binds you inextricably to all your fellow human beings.

Where then is the church of Christ to which you are called?

She is everywhere.

She holds within her all human life, and more, all heavenly beings too. For the church knows no history, her history is now, in the spiritual present.

Both family and society carry within them the tragic fate of their own limitations imposed on them by historical events. History is a time-chart of unhappiness: yet it is also the road to salvation.

But you, my young friends, are called to the church of Christ. A church conceived in God's eternity, and which carries perfection within her – just as the world carries within itself its own limited nature.

Society looks upon you as a simple building unit – one brick laid against other bricks. Your freedom in society is to function as a brick – laid once, fixed permanently.

Your only freedom in society is the freedom of constraint and in this lies your tragedy. For your real freedom lies within you. But you don't know how to find it or discern its true meaning, nor how to use it if you should discover it. You have been told that you are not free, that freedom means understanding that you are constrained and that constraint is imposed upon you from the outside. You are just like a lifeless building.

In contrast the church is alive and free. In her we live and move and have our being in Christ. In him we have full freedom. In the church we learn the truth and the truth will set us free.

You are in that church whenever you lift up someone bent down with sorrow, when you give alms to the poor, when you visit the sick. You are in Christ's church when you cry out, 'Lord help me'.

You are in Christ's church when you refuse to get angry with your neighbour – even if he has hurt your feelings! You are in Christ's church when you pray, 'Lord forgive him'.

When you work honestly at your job, and return home weary in the evenings, but with a smile on your lips – when you repay evil with love – you are in Christ's church.

Do you not see, therefore, young friends, how close the church of Christ is?

ANATOLI LEVITIN

Writer, teacher, thinker; Anatoli Levitin is all of these. Above all he is a devout Orthodox Christian. It is as a Christian that he puts the recent persecution of the Russian Orthodox Church into historical perspective for us.

Immersed as we are in the contemporary scene we may fail to realize that the present period of repression experienced by the Russian church is but one facet of the church's struggle across centuries of Russian history – a history in which the church has experienced periods of exploitation and tyranny from without, and division within.

Anatoli Levitin points out that the church lives only in Christ. A Christ who is universal – far beyond national or individual Christianity, outside history, and beyond our limited understanding of time.

Because the church lives in Christ's perpetual timelessness it never stops growing. Therefore we must look upon its suffering as growing pains.

« Growing Pains »

Jesus said, 'I am the vine, you are the branches.'

The main feature of a branch is that it grows. Growth can be an intricate, agonizing and painful process.

The church is a branch that is going out into the world from the everlasting vine, which is Christ. It is a branch extending across the whole world, spreading across centuries, a branch which becomes green and brings forth fruit as it grows – and there is no end to this growth.

The ailments of the church are growing pains.

'Then a great and mysterious sight appeared in the sky. There was a woman, whose dress was the sun and who had moons under her feet and a crown of twelve stars on her head. She was soon to give birth, and the pains and suffering of childbirth made her cry out.'

The church is like the woman in this Revelation vision, clothed with the sun. Her pains are birth pangs – for the kingdom of God is born in torment.

The ailments of the Russian church are also growing pains.

During the whole of its existence, the church in Russia has been in an abnormal position. Princes and tsars have imposed their will on it; each has leaned on it and bent it to suit himself.

Then divisions and disturbances have shaken it for twenty years of this century. After it was stained with the blood of numerous martyrs and priests in the thirties, it came under the authority of a great megalomaniac despot in the forties. He knew how to practise the inimitable art of playing on people's basest instincts – of arousing animal fear, bribing them and playing on their vanity.

Having lived again through a new period of repression, the Russian church now finds itself at a crossroads.

AN UNKNOWN BAPTIST

In a letter to a friend, the Indian philosopher Rabindranath Tagore wrote: 'After you had taken your leave, I found God's footprints on the floor.'

Issue no. 10 of the Bulletin of the Council of Prisoners' Relatives, an unofficial publication put out by Reform Baptists in the Soviet Union.

For a Christian to leave such traces behind must be the ultimate achievement.

Perhaps most of us would admit to a secret longing for some kind of immortality. Previous generations had no false modesty. The pyramids, statues, Victorian cemeteries – all bear witness to mankind's desire to leave tangible if not spiritual evidence that he passed this way.

When funerals are over, wills read, bequests made, we may have left material evidence of our earthly existence. But what evidence do we leave behind of a Christian life well lived?

A Russian Baptist asks his followers this difficult question. He is not concerned with material wealth, but spiritual riches. In true Baptist style, using metaphors familiar to country folk, he challenges apathetic Christians.

He concedes that law-abiding, respectable Christians may do no one any spiritual harm. But do they do anyone any spiritual good either?

« What Traces? »

It was night. Nature was asleep, and so was everyone in our house. Not one of us saw any rainclouds at all, nor did we hear the sound of the rain. Nevertheless, the next morning we could say that it had rained the night before since a myriad raindrops still glistened and sparkled on the trees in the grove, and puddles had appeared on the ground. All these were the visible traces left behind by the rain.

A cloud without rain leaves no such traces; it only floats across the heavens and obscures the sun, then disappears, leaving the earth as dry as before.

What a tragedy to be a Christian who just exists on the earth, unable to pour spiritual blessings on others. What a tragedy to go through life, yet leave no traces of ever having lived a Christian life.

Perhaps no one near you abuses you for being a Christian – but neither do they thank God for you. Perhaps you have never stolen money or honour from anyone. But is there a single person who has become spiritually richer for having met you? . . . You have never destroyed a single soul's faith in God – but is there anyone who has become seized with an irresistible longing for purity, holiness, truth and love – because he came to know you?

What traces are you leaving behind?

There will come a day when our earthly life will end. Heartbeats will cease. The soul will return home, the body will be buried. Only the traces of our passage through life will remain.

What will those traces be?

YAKOV SKORNYAKOV

Tourists visiting Russia may well be shown a 'registered' Baptist Church. But it's extremely unlikely that they will find themselves visiting an unregistered one. To the state authorities such churches do not exist – officially.

But exist they most certainly do – though at great cost to such as Pastor Yakov Skornyakov. Aged fifty-six, he is now serving an eight-year sentence in a strict–regime labour camp.

He is no stranger to camp life: he served a similar sentence for his religious activities from 1966 to 1971.

It was in the early 1960s that a split occurred in the Baptist church as a result of increasing state pressure: baptism of young people, Bible teaching, even the presence of children at ordinary services – all were cut back.

The only basic religious 'right' in Soviet law is the right of at least twenty adults to meet for worship in a registered building – a building where both pastor and people are restricted under state jurisdiction. Even this basic right is often denied.

A fiery, dedicated preacher, Pastor Skornyakov found this intolerable. Like many Baptists he became involved in the struggle for religious freedom, when groups of evangelical Christians formed 'unregistered' churches. This period also saw the establishment of secret printing presses – unique monuments to Russian ingenuity, concocted from scrap washing–machines and spare bicycle parts!

But Pastor Skornyakov's chief concern was for young people. Atheist local authorities could not tolerate such Christian influence. He was arrested, and began his first sentence. Following release he resumed his ministry in his church in Dzhambul. It was 1978 when he was again tried, and sent to a strict-regime camp.

Then, even before his release, due in 1983, Pastor Skornyakov was charged with continuing his Christian work among camp inmates: five of his fellow-prisoners have become committed Christians. Now, still in the camp, he is in very poor health, and has something seriously wrong with his stomach.

He is in urgent need of surgery, yet is denied medical help. In a strict-regime camp, the inadequate, often rotting food does not sustain the heavy physical labour demanded of prisoners. Yet ill as he is, Yakov Skornyakov is forced to work.

Meanwhile, back home in Dzhambul his wife Nina and their nine children wait prayerfully.

Despite his physical suffering, letters received from him demonstrate his great spiritual strength, and his longing to make Christ known to all.

'We don't need knives, pistols or any other weapons. Just as long as our God, the God of love and peace, is with us, we are strong even when we are defenceless.'

« Rain in the Valley »

I greet you in the love of the Holy Spirit. I very much want to join you in celebrating Trinity Sunday and to share with you some of my thoughts.

. . . I have been in prison this time for almost three years. I have come to the conclusion that if our godless persecutors fully understood what their persecution is doing to us they would stop it. Suffering for Christ has so much that is fine, joyous and unforgettable about it – something you might never experience in a free but humdrum existence. And then there are our heavenly rewards!

But something else worries me all the time. Nowadays the gospel is being taken in all manner of ways to the Africans, Indians, Japanese and so on. But aren't the Kazakhs, Uzbeks, Kirghiz and millions of other people in the Soviet Union sinners just as much as they are? And where can they find the gospel in their language? How and where can we preach Christ to them today?

I can't forget something that happened in 1977. A youth meeting in Talgar was broken up and the police arrested one of the leaders. During the interrogation the police chief suddenly remarked: 'You've come a long way preaching with your gospel: it's a real backwater right up in the mountains. There's nothing but bears up there!' The brother answered, 'Right, next time we'll have a meeting in the biggest park in Alma-Ata!' The police chief replied, 'That would be a breach of public order, and we'd put a stop to it even more firmly.'

'The poor and needy seek water . . .' – so Isaiah wrote.

. . . Well then, what are the poor and needy to do? Or rather, what is each of us doing already? The fact is that there are various kinds of poverty and need. Solomon says: 'One man pretends to be rich, although he has nothing.' Christ speaks even more bluntly in Revelation: 'You say, "I am rich and well off; I have all I need." But you do not know how miserable and pitiful you are! You are poor, naked and blind.'

What a horrible situation! Nothing could be worse! A man may think he is doing very well, when in fact he is on the verge of complete rejection by God.

. . . What can we do then? We, who are also poor and needy, seeking water – longing, thirsting for it? We're not talking about those who are blind, nor those people who know what their own situation is but just shrug it off. We're talking about us.

Well, we must do exactly what the first Christians did! The gospel we have is no different – it was told to us just as it was told to them.

Our Christ is no different: he is the same yesterday, today, and for ever. Our Holy Spirit is no different: his strength is not used up just because he has worked to benefit and succour all who have accepted him.

. . . When they received Christ's last command, 'Wait for the promised Holy Spirit', the disciples didn't just wander back to their own homes and their own daily affairs. They didn't just wait for things to happen. Oh no! They all gathered together in one place, and there they prayed constantly, thirsting for the fulfilment of God's promise. They gave themselves in complete obedience to him, and purified themselves physically and spiritually in preparation for dishonour, even death, in the name of the Lord Jesus.

The words of Jesus count just as much for us as for them. 'Ask and you will receive: seek and you will find.'

They discovered springs of water, but not on the safe and comfortable heights. The rain of his blessings fell on them in the valleys of tears and humiliation. Water poured out for the thirsty.

It is no different for us. But do we resemble them in our love, our self-sacrifice, our purity, our obedience, above all our longing and our thirst?

PART FIVE

CANDLES IN THE DARK

Christian courage

VLADIMIR PORESH

The Russian novelist Dostoyevsky used to say that a Russian may be a great sinner, but he will never mistake his sin for goodness. In his article 'Give your blood and receive the Spirit', Vladimir Poresh no longer feels that this is so in Russia today.

He explores, and deplores, the way people live in the Soviet Union. The atheists' conviction that men can make themselves perfect and build a perfect community has turned out to be an illusion. Christians like Vladimir believe this is because the communist system puts no value on the individual. Men and women in the Soviet Union have lost any understanding of the purpose of their lives on earth – God's purpose. Paying lip-service to empty propaganda about mankind's future harmony on earth, they carry on pointless existences seeking material goods and secure careers, and their daily life is marked by envy and suspicion of their fellow men and women.

Vladimir calls this way of life 'vulgar' – because wordly satisfaction is a sham which just disguises the fact that no true community will ever be built on atheist soil.

As a member of the 'Christian Seminar' group meeting in Moscow, Vladimir became enthused with the desire to help others understand what is lacking in Soviet life. Secure and confident in God's love, he wrote articles on this theme which were published in the Seminar's *samizdat* journal *Obshchina* ('Community').

Not concerned with merely individual holiness, Vladimir reiterates the importance of *sobornost* in the Christian life. The concept of *sobornost* is nothing new, but a longstanding idea in Russian Orthodoxy. It emphasizes freedom as the essential element of Christian love – the individual freedom which is denied by official Soviet ideology. But true freedom is not liberty to seek one's own selfish goals. It is the freedom to bind together in a loving Christian community. In a country where the ideology takes no account of the individual, *sobornost* as a living community of free individuals, poses a real threat. Those who have the courage to promote it live dangerously.

The 'Christian Seminar', an informal group of young people turning to Christ and exploring their faith, saw itself as a living example of *sobornost*: a community of individual believers united in Christian love.

In his article Vladimir challenges his readers to rethink their own idea of *sobornost* and the responsibility they have to try to bring it into existence in their lives. We who live in the West, with its general loss of inner faith and its growing obsession with outward 'vulgarity', can learn valuable lessons from him too.

« The Time For Playing Is Over »

Our revolutionary crime was the loss of a clear moral awareness, the loss of a capacity to distinguish good from evil. What a dark pit we are in now! God have mercy on us!

Our consciousness is still dimmed, our moral sense is still weak. Brute force masquerades as will-power. Some people who have begun to see clearly feel the oppressive weight of isolation – like rejected outcasts. But Christianity is a religion of power and constructive creativity.

Born and brought up in a particular culture, a man achieves freedom only by spiritual action: by acknowledging his sin and taking on the responsibility of burning the bridges behind him. The outward action, the deed, is the visible sign of deep spiritual change . . .

We all feel responsibility for the fate of our church and our homeland. We understand that we have an obligation to exercise this responsibility. We blame our parents for their helplessness, and we know the depths of our own wickedness, so we are looking for action. There is no way back. Giving up is betrayal.

God has given us a voice. With trembling hearts we accept this divine gift and pray: 'Make me a clean heart, O God; and renew a right spirit within me.'

Putting our trust in God's strength, we take up the two-edged sword of the shining gospel.

We demand normal human speech – the speech which only a clear conscience can produce. We have to reject all political activity, all calculation, everything which flourishes in this vulgar world where there is no place for truth.

Our hearts are bitter and the protest we have kept bottled up for so long is torn from us. We don't want vulgarity, the inertia that destroys. We don't want the cynicism and despair which suppresses the Word, the meaning of life. We don't want this lying peace. We want a just war. Where are you now, Holy Russia, Russia of the saints and holy men? We don't believe you are dead – only obscured by a terrible mirage.

Forgive us, Lord!

We were born in god-forsaken times. We lived as Young Pioneers and members of the *Komsomol* youth organization, but we want to die Orthodox Christians.

A longing for genuine life torments us – a life free from perversion and distortion by vulgar lies. Because this vulgarized life leads not to life but death.

Acknowledging all our inadequacy before God, we have nevertheless decided to live at any price . . .

The godless and blasphemous world of socialist realism is running away like sand between our fingers, and its dead skeleton stands naked. By our inner spiritual strength we are throwing off the fetters of a fantastic myth which has been established by the use of force. Right, truth and the redemptive suffering of our Lord Jesus Christ on the cross have shown us what genuine life really is.

A genuine perception of life is a tragic perception. But we must not run away from tragedy. We must strive for it with all our spiritual strength, for tragedy is the opposite of everyday vulgarity, just as truth is the opposite of the lie. We must open our hearts to meet suffering.

The Christian belief in the incarnation means that when Christ became man he became God, and therefore truth, in human form – and that he remains truth. It is a necessary consequence of this belief that we should manifest one of the main ideas of the Orthodox Church – the idea of *sobornost*. We must act in such a way that our faith does not simply become a matter of inner contemplation, cut off from life, but becomes active and incarnate in our life.

History is a conversation between God and man – a continuing revelation. Every one of us receives his own personal revelation. Every one of us must make a concrete and substantial response.

> 'The time for playing is over;
> Flowers do not bloom twice.
> The shadow of the giant mountain
> Has fallen across our path.'

AN ANONYMOUS CATHOLIC

Half praying, half thinking aloud, an anonymous Catholic from Czechoslovakia addresses God as his spiritual sounding-board and confidant.

He is a frightened man, deeply aware of his own shortcomings and those of his church. We all like to air our doubts and grievances when we feel insecure. The author of this excerpt is no exception.

This whole excerpt endears us to the writer. There is little doubt that he feels better by the end of his communion with God. There are touches of wry humour, and an altogether more positive attitude is revealed as he reassures himself and his fellow Christians of God's enduring love and support.

Direct, humble, inspired with complete faith, this piece of writing is not easy to categorize. Is it prayer, thinking aloud, meditation or intercession? It is difficult to name it neatly. But one thing is certain. It is a fine example of one man's communication with his God in a contemporary situation – a situation in which Christian courage is challenged daily.

« Spirit of Caution »

God of strength, God of might . . .

How often, Lord, I turn to you with this Good Friday cry. It is because I am afraid, and fear is so unpleasant.

The cover of 'Spektrum', an unauthorized literary and philosophical journal put out by Roman Catholics in Czechoslovakia.

I hear well-meaning unbelievers say, 'It's all right for you Christians, you've got God, you're not afraid!' But others often say quite the reverse: 'You Christians never seem to show any moral strength! We expect you to fight in the front line – especially in religious matters. Instead you shrink back in fear.'

Dear God, the spirit of caution usually wins with us Catholics in Czechoslovakia! But isn't caution the virtue which prevents courage turning into defiant insolence? Tell me though, what use is caution where there is no courage, or where the bold power of love should be greater? We are all witnesses to the lies and injustices, the physical annihilation and moral destruction going on around us. Yet who has opposed it?

Dear God, I know there are timorous souls whom one can't ask to join battle. I pray for them and ask you to give them a true spirit of prayer that they may pray twice as fervently and support those in the thick of the fray.

God give me the gift of discernment. It is not always through timidity that we go astray. A lot of people believe that we are the suffering church – that meekness is more fitting than protest. Were the prophets, martyrs, and bishops of old wrong then to defend justice and freedom and champion the cause of the oppressed and the persecuted? Their deeds are part of the church's glorious tradition. But the attitude taken by those followers of Christ who remain silent and turn aside from their responsibilities is deeply depressing.

How many excuses they invent, each more pious than the last, to evade your call and that of their fellow men. Where is the strength of the early Christians? . . . They never rendered to Caesar what belonged only to God.

Is this why the words 'holy and strong' no longer go together? Are we weak because we are not holy? We have no saints, only sanctimonious men and women.

You don't promise us an easy life; but rather suffering and death. But you did promise us that through such trials we would achieve blessedness. You told us to rejoice when we were persecuted for your name's sake.

What has become of our joy?

What consternation and panic there is when someone is summoned for interrogation! Where is our pride in suffering for your sake? Are we the church militant?

No! we are the church in flight.

We complain that our church has no rising generation. Who would want to join such cowards?

Let us show ourselves spiritually strong – then we shall have a new generation. We have no young people because we are so petty and narrow-minded. O God increase our faith and trust in you!

Lord, you were willing to spare Sodom and Gomorrah for the sake of ten righteous men. I imagine that we must have more than ten since we have escaped annihilation! I thank you for them. Bless them, and multiply their number!

. . . The apostles joyfully bore witness to the risen Christ. If a Christian is to be a witness he must not be afraid to speak out for fear of provoking negative reactions from his listeners.

If he fails to bear witness, he denies his calling. He then

ceases to be a Christian . . . for faith, this wonderful plant, thrives only on action, on witnessing to the outside world.

While doing this, the Christians must endure all difficulties. A Christian must never give up . . For above all he has the love of God, from which no power in heaven or earth can separate him.

ANATOLI LEVITIN

Anatoli Levitin has a well-stocked mind. He illuminates thorny questions that many Christians wish to evade. But he spices erudite exposition with snippets of history and literary allusion. Here he tackles the question of Christian courage and strength.

Levitin does not write about courage lightly. For he has faced imprisonment and persecution for his beliefs. Like the apostle Paul before him he knows all about courage, and the lack of it.

In this essay on the true essence of Christianity, Levitin seeks to correct what he sees as a mistake made by the church in Russia. It is a traditional Orthodox belief that meekness is one of the greatest Christian virtues. But has this made the church a slave of the Russian state?

Historically the church in Russia always supported the Russian rulers and emperors. And in the early days it was in its own interests to do so, since otherwise Russia and its culture would have been destroyed by the Tartars.

However, such allegiance bred too much servility, says Levitin. Fawning bishops nourished meekness in the church. But meekness degenerated into cowardice and egoism. The church became weak through its close involvement with the state, and lost its nerve.

Eventually, says Levitin, the Russian people began to believe that slavish submissiveness was almost a synonym for Christianity.

Anatoli Levitin knows that this traditional view of meekness may still be found in conservative Russian Orthodoxy today. But he warns us that the other extreme is equally dangerous – an inflated view of your own importance. Pride leads to rivalry and sets men against each other and against God. The safeguard against this is that strength must always be tempered with love – this is the safeguard given us in Christianity.

« Put Love First »

What must we do to reveal the true essence of Christianity?

For this it is necessary first of all to be courageous, and turning to the gospel, throw away all the layers which have encrusted it over the centuries.

In the Old Testament the Lord blesses spiritual strength and the will to struggle. He is the Lord of victories, terrible and strong. Strength of will and spiritual power are the image and likeness of God in man.

The Old Testament is fire – clear and convincing. And what can be simpler and stronger than fire?

The New Testament is different. It is fire, and water, and strength, and blue sky.

The Old Testament is nationalistic, with one voice and one theme. It is easy to see the opposite shore when you stand on the bank of a lake. But try to make out the opposite shore of an ocean. It's not just difficult, it's impossible. There is nothing for it but to cross the ocean.

The Old Testament is like a fiery seething lake. The New Testament is an ocean, sometimes calm, sometimes stormy. It is hard to be mistaken in what we see clearly on the other side of a lake. But it's easy to deceive ourselves and others about the other side of an ocean.

It is only human to over-simplify complicated phenomena which are difficult to understand, and so vulgarization permeates every sphere of human activity. We have vulgarized science, vulgarized art and vulgarized ideology.

There is also vulgarized Christianity. For example, the sham humility that is preached and encouraged by the princes of the church who demand humility and meekness from others but never practice it themselves. This vulgarized Christianity, sentimentalized and emasculated, has nothing in common with genuine Christianity.

Real Christianity is not weakness, but strength. Not whining, but preaching. It's not a whisper but a proclamation. Real Christianity never accommodates falsehood and violence but exposes and rejects those who seek to devalue it. It is not death but life, not peace but a sword.

At the same time Christianity is the cross. It is suffering for the truth. It is love . . .

Now I shall speak again and again about love. Without love everything fades and grows dim, even virtue and truth itself . . .

Piety without love is bombastic nonsense. Neither God nor man needs it. Meekness without love is servility and fawning. Even a bold spirit without love is a mercenary and a cutthroat.

But here a new temptation arises. Pride. Pride is not an invention of certain moral theologians. It's a fact of life. But what is pride?

Pride is will, but will without love. And will without love leads man to vain self-glory – to considering himself superior to others.

One of the most brilliant works of the nineteenth century is Ibsen's *Brand*. The hero of the drama is an inflexible pastor, a bold and incorruptible exposer of evil and vice. He comes out openly against the powerful men of this world, and draws general hatred down upon himself. He loses his post and is left entirely alone. Even his loving wife abandons him.

For him this is the end. He goes into the mountains. An avalanche of snow is moving towards him. In a moment it will fall and crush him. It's at this moment that Brand challenges God.

'Oh God! At least answer me in the last hour of my life.'

With a roar the avalanche crashes down and buries Brand. Because Brand does not love, he is defeated in his struggle with God.

Will without love is nothing but pride.

TRAIAN DORZ

When Traian Dorz was tried in Romania for distributing religious literature, his prosecutors confessed themselves puzzled. 'Why do you continue to produce and circulate religious literature when you have already spent so many years in prison?'

Traian's reply was characteristic:

'There are so few Bibles in Romania, and as long as not everyone who wants one has one, I will continue to encourage people to bring them to us, and I will give away as many as I can.'

His stand is typical of those Romanian Orthodox believers who are members of 'The Lord's Army'. Rejected by their own church, they continue to grow in spiritual fervour and purpose. They now number at least half a million members, many of whom are peasants and young people. All are determined to renew the spiritual life of Romania and protect it from the tyranny of state control. Many Orthodox priests express sympathy with the aims of 'The Lord's Army' and are themselves castigated by their own hierarchy for disloyalty to the 'state' church.

As a prolific writer and committed member of this movement, Traian Dorz was convinced of the power of the printed word as an evangelistic tool.

In this poem he shares his understanding of true Christian charity, forgiveness and acceptance of God's will.

« The Price »

Though so many have deceived me,
I do not ever want to say
that I no longer trust in men,
or that I in turn break with them.

For many were my friends
more precious than pure gold.
And so many, through the slime of the world,
have kept themselves whiter than snow.
Many the Word have kept
at whatever the price,
preserving the road of faith
with the sacrifice of their own lives.
Thus I do not break off from men
because many were villains.
For God among them yet
has his treasures and his angels.

PART SIX

SUFFERING IN THE LIGHT

Prisons and trials

VLADIMIR PORESH

C. S. Lewis once said of friendship that it has no survival value; rather it is one of those things that give value to survival.

There is no doubt that to a young Christian standing trial in Soviet Russia for disseminating his religious beliefs, the prospect of survival must have seemed bleak. Yet for Vladimir Poresh the experience proved to have enormous value just because of his friends' love and prayers.

A surprising number of students around today's world come to experience a religious conversion. In the West some may greet this with a wry smile, but the students will not be hounded for their beliefs by the state.

For Vladimir it was different.

He was born in 1949 to intellectual parents – both members of the party. He grew into a gangling adolescent. A kind, trusting boy, he never questioned his parents' atheism.

And yet – as he reached his late teens he wondered. What was life really all about? He argued and questioned. He studied, finally going to Leningrad University.

Once there, homesick and alone, he experienced great uncertainty. Life seemed utterly meaningless. But like a true scholar he gradually began to search for a meaning. And the more he thought and studied the more deeply he changed. Slowly, he came to acknowledge that God exists – but a sure faith was slow to develop.

And then he met Alexander.

Alexander Ogorodnikov was a committed young Christian. He acted like a catalyst on Vladimir's tentative faith. Within months of their meeting in 1973 Vladimir was baptized into the Orthodox church. Then the work really began.

Together, he and Alexander founded the Christian Seminar in Moscow. The group met in Alexander's flat which was little

Tanya Poresh and her two daughters have had to wait many years for Vladimir to be released from prison. Prisoners' families bear a heavy burden.

more than a shed. It was cold, yet full of Christian warmth. About two dozen young men and women met regularly there to discuss their faith. Out of these discussions the little typewritten journal *Obshchina* ('Community') was born.

It was the birth of this humble publication which finally broke the Seminar. The KGB pounced. Vladimir was arrested. On 1 August 1979 he was sentenced to five years' imprisonment followed by three years' exile. He was just thirty.

At his trial the courtroom was packed. His friends listened spellbound to his impassioned plea for their cause. As he was sentenced, a great shout rang round the hall, 'Volodya we love you!' As they sang 'Christ is Risen', he knew that his trial was not a defeat but a victory for all of them.

This is part of his defence at that trial.

« Such Joy There Is »

Again and again I have asked for an explanation. Where, and in what way, can these writings and documents be called anti-Soviet? Certainly I have never denied the facts of this case, but I cannot agree with the court's assessment of my activities, or my motives. The indictment says the material is slanderous – yet not one reason, not a single detail, is given for this view. It is merely the personal opinion of the investigators.

I am a Christian. Just as Marxism-Leninism has a complete world-view, so I have a world-view . . . But mine is based on Christianity and the church.

How, therefore, can I be expected to help the state to build up Communism? It is not my job to help create a society without God.

Ever since the Soviet regime was established believers have been persecuted. As for the clergy, thousands of priests have been shot. When their martydom is honoured, their icons painted, will that be considered anti-soviet activity too?

Even now, every day, Christians are outraged by the constant stream of atheist propaganda. Everywhere our state scorns religion as the 'opium of the people'. The people themselves are then exhorted to 'crush this foul creature'.

When Comrade Procurator asked me if I had been harassed at work I had to say "No, I have not". But I was there on Mayakovsky Street when seminar members were arrested – and on other occasions when they were persecuted.

It is true that when I was held for questioning I was offered the chance to receive holy communion – for this I must be thankful. But it alters nothing. The persecution of believers in Russia still goes on.

I am charged with working to influence people. Surely all writers do – but I have never called for struggle against the State. I have always had a negative attitude towards Soviet power, but I have never encouraged anyone to fight against it.

During my trial my letter to Alexander Solzhenitsyn was mentioned. In that letter I showed my conviction that the best way to struggle against Soviet power is not to struggle against it at all! Rather it is better to be positive, to be creative in our efforts to assert our faith in all its strength.

When I wrote in my letter to Solzhenitsyn that I saw his books as a positive call to action please understand that I was talking here of spiritual action. I must emphasize this point. The whole aim of our journal, and my personal aim, was to bring Christianity to the world and to free people from the social pressures which restrict them.

I have written about this to friends in France and Italy . . . In countries which still enjoy democracy and freedom Christians still have to fight existing social pressures. We all have one common struggle: the struggle to liberate society from social evils.

. . . The indictment states that in my letter to Solzhenitsyn I called for action by any means against Soviet power. Now let me tell you what I actually wrote:

"Dear Alexander Isayevich,

Please put us in contact with other religious communities or groups of young people like ourselves in the USA or other countries. We are in sympathy with believers in the widest sense."

I said the same thing in my letter to young people in the

West. This is our main task: to create a Christian fellowship transcending all national boundaries.

And in fact it is my view of the world which I am being sentenced for. Obviously in a totalitarian state I am breaking the law by holding an individual point of view on this . . . I really do not see how I could have avoided prison. After all, I have always acted quite naturally on my convictions. I have never tried to hide anything. If I had been a law-abiding citizen I would have kept my mouth shut and stayed at home.

But for a Christian this is not good enough. We cannot just quietly practise our religious rituals. We cannot stop there, we must go further. We need the world . . .

So now you have the facts. You have heard the whole case. I do not intend to overturn the law, which has been administered in accordance with a socialist view of justice. I am not asking for special treatment. It is not my way. The Procurator asked for a short sentence for me. I would have asked for a longer one – though I know that I do not deserve that privilege, for others have done far more for the church than I have.

You have seen the witnesses. All of them are my friends; believers and unbelievers. Such joy there is in their faces! It was a joy for them to see me and joy for me to see them. This whole hall has been filled with a constant feeling of joy even though I stand here as a prisoner.

Many of the witnesses have helped me even when they did not completely share my convictions. We see here a new religious community. These are my friends. They are also soldiers of Christ and they will win the world for his church.

This new awareness of God at work through Christians everywhere is becoming a reality – a spiritual fact. Yes, even here in this very courtroom the idea has been created.

It has made me realize that this must have been the meaning and purpose of this whole trial. That is why I am happy to accept my sentence.

MIKHAIL KHOREV

As prisoners are loaded into trucks and driven away to labour camp, their families know that they will be separated for many

years. They know too that their loved one will be poorly housed, poorly fed and frequently ill with exhaustion.

But what of the wives and many children left behind? Theirs is a sad story too, for they also have to undergo hardship, cold and hunger.

The wives and families of Soviet political prisoners receive no support of any kind from the state. And such work as a mother may find is often menial and poorly paid as the relatives of these prisoners are frequently hounded and denied skilled employment. Under the Soviet system there are no charitable organizations independent of the state, so that the families of Christian prisoners are dependent on the support of fellow-believers. In addition, children can suffer discrimination at school and in the job market.

Perhaps the saddest aspect of a family's poverty is that often they cannot scrape together enough money to pay a prisoner the rare visits he is allowed. The cost of travel to the purposely inaccessible labour camps is often prohibitive. And even when a visit is arranged, wives may be subjected to humiliating interrogation and are sometimes strip-searched.

We can only marvel at the faith and solidarity of such families as Mikhail Khorev's. Not once but several times, he and his family suffered through his imprisonment.

Mikhail Khorev, now fifty-three, is a Baptist pastor from Kishinyov in Moldavia. A member of the unregistered Baptist church, he went as a delegate to Moscow in 1966. There, during a demonstration seeking religious freedom, he was arrested. Tried and imprisoned, he was put under tremendous pressure to collaborate with the authorities. He refused, stating that he would rather spend all his life in prison than betray his church. Now he is back in labour camp. Not long ago he wrote a letter to President Brezhnev listing oppressive measures at the camp. He resolved to fast until he received a reply. The guards retaliated by force-feeding him.

Mikhail Khorev's current sentence is for five years' strict-regime camp. He was charged with 'disrupting public order'. His crime? Holding meetings in the forest and in people's homes for prayer, hymn singing and Bible study!

'Of course I would gladly go home to my family today if the court would allow me,' he said at his trial. 'My family and my home are dear to me; in this respect I am just like you. My children are dear to me, and my wife. But I know that today I shall spend the night on a bare board and I shall continue to eat prison broth. I choose this of my own free will because I never intend to betray my Lord.'

« The Bouquet »

I will never forget the day when I received my first prison term for service to my Lord. When the sentence was read out to me, the courtroom was full of people. Friends encouraged me saying: 'The Lord will bless you: take heart, stand firm.'

So now I knew how many years I would be in the camp, how old my children would be when I returned home . . . But nothing could compare with the enduring impression of the presence of my friends at the trial. What cheerfulness of spirit, what joy in their faces! They promised to pray for me and I was prepared to meet any hardship with joy. But the Lord had still more comfort in store for me that day.

The police van drove up. A lot of prisoners were already sitting inside. I heard words of greeting, and flowers were flung towards me, but I was ordered to hold my hands behind my back. As I walked, I tried not to step on any of the flowers, but even so there were many underfoot. My eyes filled with tears, not from sorrow at parting, but from a deep, holy trembling.

'I am not worthy, Lord,' I thought, 'of your mercy.'

Through a living tunnel of militia men, I entered the police van – the last man in. They didn't close the grilled door quickly enough, and someone threw a well-aimed bouquet of flowers after me. From behind the bars, the prisoners' hands reached out to the scattered blooms and gathered them up. There were enough flowers for everyone to have one except me

– I was left with the string which had tied up the bouquet. The prisoners were all talking among themselves: everyone had his own tale to tell about his trial, and nobody asked once who the flowers had been meant for.

After a quarter of an hour the police van arrived at the courthouse in another district, and a young woman was put in with us. The men, like savages, cried 'Hurrah!' and many ribald remarks ensued. The woman was not timid either, and responded with choice abuse. They put her in a little cell next to us, called a 'box', where it is only possible to sit – you can't stand up. And the conversation began again, 'What are you in for?' and so on.

Suddenly someone jokingly suggested, 'Come on boys! Let's collect the flowers and give them to our lady.'

Everyone quickly passed his flower back through the bar. They put the bouquet together again, and said to the escort who was accompanying the vehicle, 'Give these to our neighbour.'

Just to be kind, apparently, he opened the door a crack and handed her the bouquet.

Surprised, she asked, 'Where did you get such beautiful flowers, lads?'

'We don't know, they were thrown to somebody.'

'Come on, whose flowers are these?' she insisted.

'They're my flowers,' I heard myself say.

'Why don't you keep them, then?'

'Friends gave them to me, but I didn't catch them.'

'What are you in for? People don't get given flowers after their trial!'

'It looks as though my trial was the exception.'

'So what are you in for?' she repeated.

'For service to the Lord; I am a Christian.'

At once a lively conversation began. They started asking me dozens of questions about the Holy Scriptures. The woman, it turned out, was sharing her cell with another who was a believer.

She stopped using foul language, and asked, 'What kind of job did you have in the church?'

'I am a pastor,' I answered.

Then she told me, 'Promise me that you will pray for me this very day. I'm a human being too, and I need that salvation which your believing sister has been telling me about. I was brought up in a children's home, and I've only just heard about God. I want to have eternal life too. Tell me, is it true what she told me, that God forgives all sin?'

Some of the prisoners began to laugh, but she said to me through the wall, 'Pay no attention to them. I laughed too when I knew no better.'

Serious now, she went on: 'Lads, please, treat this man with special respect, shake his hand for me. I'd do it myself if only there wasn't this partition between us.'

Then, as if coming to her senses, she said, 'Why is there such injustice? Why were the flowers given to me? They belong to you.'

She called the escort, and pleaded with him: 'Give him the flowers, please!'

He said 'Come on, make up your minds, what d'you think I am, a yoyo?'

But she insisted: 'If you want to do something nice for someone for once, I beg you, even if you ignore everything else we ask, at least do this one thing, please.'

She pleaded so persuasively that the escort gave in. He opened the door a crack, took the flowers through the bars, and gave them to me.

They were no longer anything like the fresh bouquet which my friends had thrown me. But I took the string from my pocket and lovingly tied them up.

'Please, give us your farewell blessing.'

'May Jesus Christ, who is able to save in all circumstances, be with you always.' Everyone said, 'Thank you!'

I left with the bouquet in my hands. The police van had stopped right in front of a gate which could only be opened from the inside. The escort rang a bell. An officer opened the gate and, a convict for the first time in my life, I entered the prison holding the crushed and limp bouquet. 'What's the meaning of this, coming into the prison with flowers?' asked the officer.

'Friends gave them to me,' I replied.

'Coming in here with flowers is forbidden. Throw them away,' he ordered. So I carefully put the flowers in the waste-bin just as they would normally be arranged in a proper flower vase.

After my release, I went specially to this entrance to the prison. There, deeply moved, I stood for a long time at the spot where I had once laid the bouquet of flowers which had been so dear to me. Though they had been discarded like rubbish, the whole event had been significant to me. The Lord had wonderfully encouraged me at the most difficult moment of my life.

I often wonder where that woman is now who needed my prayer of blessing. I haven't seen her since that day, but I do know that a good seed, by God's grace, produces an abundance of shoots. I may meet her again in the kingdom of heaven.

FRANTISEK LIZNA

Stone walls do not a prison make,
Nor iron bars a cage;
Minds innocent and quiet take
That for an hermitage.

These words might have been written for Frantisek Lizna. Like John Bunyan, and the apostle Paul before him, the captivity which confined his body released his mind into fresh spiritual dimensions. Here in the pages of his letters from prison Frantisek distils his joy, his wisdom and perception of God. These are passages to treasure, to read again and again. Here is a man with a gift for turning the most negative circumstances into positive opportunities –even the dust in his cell inspires him to praise God.

Frantisek was born in Czechoslovakia in 1947. Life for a Christian is very difficult under the Communist regime in that country. All monastic orders were dissolved in 1950. Priests are now virtually civil servants. Their ministry is monitored, and anything but mediocrity punished.

Against this background young Frantisek grew up. As a teenager he was sentenced for pulling down a Soviet flag. From that day he became a marked man, for ever in and out of prison for 'activities against the state'.

During his prison sentences he met and was greatly influenced by imprisoned priests. It was 1974 when he too became a priest.

Even without his prison record, his spiritual enthusiasm would have singled him out. It is a wonder the authorities allowed him to go to theological college, let alone become a priest.

Then, on the day he celebrated his first mass – the crowning moment in a priest's life – the blow fell. His licence was revoked. Permission to officiate was never granted again. He worked instead as a medical orderly.

In 1981, and again in 1982, he was further sentenced for 'damaging state interests abroad'.

Since his imprisonment Fr Lizna has written several letters to his family and friends. A priest without a parish, without even the right to say mass, he has ministered instead to a whole country through his writing. Shut away, he is banned now from writing or even receiving letters himself; but his much-loved bundle of letters circulates still in Czechoslovakia, inspiring all who read them.

« Grains of Dust »

28 March

Although we can't leave our cell except for short walks, we are not alone. I know the Lord cares for us far more than if we were surrounded by wealth and acclaim. Wealth and human acclaim are only worldy and fleeting anyway.

What I live on is hope. This hope is invincible. It is the only thing which is real since nothing in the world can undermine

Fr Frantisek Lizna celebrates his first mass after ordination as priest. It was to be his only one. His licence was revoked by the authorities that very day.

it. The more you read about Marxist philosophy and the laws of history, the more gaps and flaws you find in the arguments. At this moment I am thinking particularly of you, standing amidst your flower beds, exhausted by hard work. You won't have the time or energy to read such sophisticated writings. You should never cease thanking God for your lot – that would make me very happy.

Those of us who live restless and hurried lives need to be brought up short from time to time by the constant presence of the sick in their wheelchairs and those who nurse them so devotedly, in order to remember where we come from. We must remember where we are going, too. It's so easy to forget that we have been chosen for one end, especially when our eyes rest on the glowing colours of the world around us. Yet if we look more closely we can see that where these colours fade there is only drab greyness underneath. We are in danger of leading such hectic lives, full of worldly distractions, that we fail to grow spiritually, and this is fatal. At least that can't happen in here. Thank the Lord!

It's frightening what prison reveals! Men who are cornered lose the last shreds of human decency. It's agony for me to realize that the truth is revealed through suffering, but at the same time I'm glad that I'm less naive. May God keep me on the right path.

I am sure that St Francis would talk to this cell as if it were a living thing. He'd be sorry for it enduring so much foul language from its inhabitants as they kick the walls mercilessly. Honestly it's not bad. I moved here from somewhere much worse. It's large, light, and remarkably warm – it even lets in some spring air. It's nothing like as gloomy as you imagine. Do give thanks to God for this, and for caring for us so well.

During the night, whenever I wake up, I do as you once suggested. I pray for those who have died and who are suffering because they have cut themselves off from God's love. Since I pray as a priest, I don't feel alone, but full of health and joy. Don't be afraid, I don't forget any of you, who belong to me. I just ask that you should thank God for looking after us so well, preparing everything down to the last detail.

Isn't it amazing? After two years living in Prague, I had to come to a place like this to hear a bird singing right under my window. Not just one bird either, but the whole dawn chorus.

Though I often dwell in the past – especially remembering my visits to Osterley and Carinthia – I share every moment of my present with God. And at present I am in this cell, which was given to me free to live in without my having to bribe the housing authorities.

I've come to look on this cell as a secret friend, and refuse to treat her badly. Maybe it's for this reason I've been kept here for so long . . .

12 April

Today is Easter Monday. I know my letter will arrive late but I must greet you all with a joyous Alleluia – for Christians can express joy in the resurrection at any time, in any situation. The Bible tells us that Christians radiate this joy even when

The Bible tells us that Christians radiate this joy even when about to be eaten by the lions – so much so, that even the lions hesitate. This pure happiness is given freely by God, it's part of his victory and glory. There will be no joy without our willingness to share what the church has yet to endure, but suffering and joy are so carefully balanced that I know we are in the hands of our merciful Lord.

I received letters from you and my sister on Good Friday. I saved them up for a special treat to read early in the morning on Easter Day. What a beautiful night! As I read I felt I was really with you all – it seemed as if we were travelling the road to Emmaus together. I almost apologized to my warder for my absence! All the time, of course, I was really down on my knees before our risen Lord. Alleluia.

25 April

A beautiful morning! The sunshine in our cell assures us that God never forgets us. He pours down light on everyone, good and evil alike. How quietly the sun fills the room – quite different from the way we human beings behave. Its strong, delicate rays carefully illumine every grain of dust. We're no longer alone. I'd love to greet every particle of dust – here hated by everyone. I'm grateful that they're here. They show how something normally despised can be tansfigured into something beautiful. Look how each grain sparkles! The grace to see God's glory has been given to me here in prison. No longer will dust irritate me. Instead it will remind me of my cell and stimulate me to wonder at God's creation.

16 June

You who work among the sick know too well that suffering is part and parcel of life. I think with love of all Christians who have suffered. Their pain is a living sacrifice. They have suffered quietly, humbly, in secret, and their sufferings are brought in prayer before our invisible God. But at the same time their sufferings are the reality on which our world rests – because without Calvary our world would be damned. But all this is too theological for now. I will take refuge in the simple prayer, 'Come Holy Spirit'. Say it with me now!

I have also prayed for our neighbour Poland. It's wonderful to hear that someone there remembered to pray for me too.

I almost forgot that I'm still in Prague. This is when I realize that it's not where but how we live that matters. Let's invoke the Holy Spirit, who can melt all prison bars, for we know that the strongest bars are not made of steel but of hard and cruel hearts.

Come Holy Spirit, come!

INTRODUCING CHRISTIANS IN LITHUANIA

A number of the pieces that follow are by Lithuanians. What sort of people are they?

Of all the Soviet republics the small Baltic state of Lithuania might be considered the thorn in the flesh of the USSR.

Lithuania is unique in the Soviet Union, for its population is almost wholly Roman Catholic, with a brand of Catholicism that is fervently nationalistic. Like their neighbours in Poland, the Lithuanian people have maintained fierce opposition to their communist masters. To Lithuanians the Russians are an occupying nation. The Russian language is imposed on the people, and Russians occupy many key government and political posts.

Unlike the churches in many other Eastern-bloc countries, the church in Lithuania draws together young and old in an almost total opposition to the atheistic regime. Members of the church hierarchy have only rarely been heard to advise dissenting priests and people not to rock the boat – instead all continue to rock the boat together. The Roman Catholic church in the Soviet Union is allowed no central administrative bodies, so the Lithuanian church draws hope and spiritual support direct from the Vatican.

On the accession of Pope John Paul II, priests in Lithuania sent a greetings telegram assuring him of their support. The Pope replied with a message in which he 'lovingly thanked and blessed his greatly beloved church in Lithuania'. As a token of his love and support he sent his Cardinal's hat which is now treasured in the Vilnius church of Ausros Vartai

The Hill of Crosses has become an important shrine for Lithuanian Christians. Put up by ordinary believers, the crosses are often removed by the authorities, only to be replaced by further crosses.

the *samizdat* press carried an article headlined, 'We are strong because we are not alone'!

The clampdown on *samizdat* publications in the USSR generally results in their demise. But the *Chronicle of the Lithuanian Catholic Church* has remained in print and flourishes still. A powerful weapon in the fight for human rights and religious liberty, it is now well known in the West, and no doubt keeps the Vatican informed of Catholic suffering in Lithuania. It was first issued in 1972. Many who were instrumental in launching it have suffered persecution by the authorities. Key figures such as Petras Plumpa, Vladas Lapienis and Nijole Saduniate were given harsh sentences and endured great physical and spiritual suffering in labour camps. They typify the stamina and sacrifice of Lithuanians in their struggle to preserve their faith for the future.

VIKTORAS PETKUS

When Viktoras Petkus became a member of the Lithuanian Helsinki Monitoring Group it was obvious that his days of freedom would be numbered.

It was in December 1976 that a Lithuanian group was set up to monitor observance of the Helsinki Agreement. Once again Lithuanian nationalist and Catholic zeal proved itself, for while similar groups in Russia were liquidated, the Lithuanian group survived until quite recently. Closely linked with the *Chronicle of the Lithuanian Catholic Church*, and disseminating to the West statements about the violation of religious rights, all those involved became obvious targets for the KGB.

Viktoras Petkus was arrested for the third time in 1977 and sentenced the following year to a horrific total of fifteen years' imprisonment, strict-regime camp and exile.

The manner of his arrest, and the charges against him, were particularly unjust. As a nationalist, a committed Catholic and a youth worker he was especially vulnerable. Accusations made against him included inciting young people to go to church, to form gangs, and to indulge in 'riotous drunken orgies'! Even worse, four schoolboys were put under pressure to sign statements that Viktoras was homosexual and had assaulted them. All four refused to give such evidence, and all four were expelled from school. Now fifty-four, Viktoras Petkus endures the rigours of a strict-regime camp. Always his great comforter, Jesus Christ, sustains him. And always he tries to pass on the knowledge of God's love to his fellow-prisoners, some of whom are hardened criminals. Like so many Christians persecuted for their beliefs, Viktoras lives in the present moment and uses every opportunity to commend Jesus. In a letter home he recounts one of the most moving experiences in his life.

'I have been doing quite well during the past year. I was given a beautiful memento by over forty thieves and other fellow-prisoners. When Pope Paul died they asked me to tell them about the Pope and explain the differences between the Catholic and Orthodox religions. I tried to do what they asked . . .

'They were so quiet and listened for hours on end with the greatest interest. Afterwards they overwhelmed me with questions! I'll never forget how later some of them gathered together in a corner. There they unravelled a nylon sock, and were busy working away at something all afternoon.

'It was after supper when they came to me and presented me with a cross carefully made out of all those nylon threads. They then thanked me for sharing my knowledge with them.

'I have probably never received a more precious gift in my life!'

Not for nothing is Lithuania known as 'The Land of Crosses'. To a devout Catholic people the cross means a great deal – the Lithuanians erect crosses on their hills, in the countryside, and in their gardens. They wear crosses, and they place them in their houses as an ever-present reminder of Christ crucified and their own participation in his suffering.

It showed special sensitivity and genuine courage on the part of his fellow-prisoners when they unravelled a precious sock to make Viktoras a cross of his very own.

« Homeland's Forests »

I have somehow become accustomed to my surroundings. In gratitude to divine Providence, I repeat a prayer every night that I learned thirty years ago:

You come through thick stone walls, armed guards and bars: you bring me a starry night and ask about this and that. You are the Redeemer. I recognize you. You are my way, my truth and my life. Even my cellar blooms with stars, and peace and light pour fourth. You sprinkle beautiful words on me like flowers: 'Son, what are you afraid of? I am with you!'

I received your February 20 letter on May 19. Perhaps my letter will also take three months to reach you . . . It is not much better with letters written in Russian . . .

In February I sent a fifty-two page letter on the influence of certain philosophical ideas on Lithuanian literature. Early in April I was told that my letter was confiscated for so-called 'ideologically harmful expressions'.

I am very sorry that I lack the opportunity to answer diligently the letters I receive, but my hands are tied by the 'quota'. Good people understand this and patiently continue to write even though they receive no news from me. Those letters bring me a breath of air from the homeland and the whisper of the pines on Birute's Hill, the sound of pilgrims singing hymns and the poet's words:

'Whoever bears my Calvaries will celebrate my feast of joy.'

With the poet I also would like to wish:

'May the words ring out, like the rustle of my homeland's forest. May they echo in the hearts of living Lithuanians.'

PETRAS PLUMPA

'If God doesn't exist why should anyone fight against him?'

Young Petras Plumpa often asked himself this question when he was serving a prison sentence in 1958. A teenage tearaway, he had been imprisoned for seven years for alleged nationalist activities – based merely on his possession of rusty militaria collected in the Second World War.

In prison he became disillusioned with nationalism alone, and sought for a deeper meaning to life. He learned French and read the French philosophers in the prison library. But philosophy failed to give him an answer, although it raised many questions in his mind. Gradually, like many in prison before him, he discovered faith.

On his release he looked for ways to serve God. The way he found was to launch and produce the *Chronicle of the Lithuanian Catholic Church*. A *samizdat* publication, it has enormous influence and aims to tell the truth about violations of religious rights. The KGB went to great lengths to suppress it and arrested Petras and his colleagues in 1974.

He faced appalling conditions during his sentence. He was beaten up by murderers and thieves who stole his padded coat

and warm gloves. His guards victimized him even more cruelly, manhandling and bullying him. They even stole his prayer book and his pictures of Jesus. Petras was barred from writing or receiving letters for months at a time. Eventually his wife was allowed to see him. But she was stripped naked and searched: she was not allowed to give him any paper or writing materials.

Petras' health was very poor in camp, yet medical treatment was withheld for his high blood-pressure and eye infection. Despite everything his Christian courage held firm. Not once did he waver in his faith, believing as he did that Christians of today should follow Christ in suffering.

This passage is from a letter he wrote while in prison.

« Let Us Bloom In Sorrow »

No matter where we may live the same important problems and questions always arise – about the salvation of souls – and it is not always easy to know the most suitable field for us, where we could bring most benefit. Only the King of souls knows that. We are left to bloom where he has sown us.

If he has sown us in the field of sorrows – let us bloom in sorrow. If he has sown us in solitude, let it be solitude, for the Creator sows even the most beautiful of flowers on inaccessible tracks between mountain paths, and they have their value even though nobody sees them. In these days it is impossible for us to live without being seen: only the anguish of the soul can be unseen, and like blossoms it can be constantly plucked and offered to the Saviour. This is the most beautiful decoration for the altar of Jesus. Without decorations of this kind even the finest churches are sad places: without that kind of donor even the greatest of nations is poverty-stricken.

NIJOLE SADUNAITE

'She'd walk around the women's camp singing at the top of her voice – to cheer up the men in their camp nearby. Everybody liked her. She could even charm the guards into carrying messages from the women over to the men.'

This endearing picture of Nijole Sadunaite was painted by one of her fellow-prisoners at the labour camp in Mordovia.

Nijole Sadunaite was a young Lithuanian woman when she was arrested in 1974 for making typewritten copies of the *Chronicle of the Lithuanian Catholic Church.*

Sentenced in 1975 to three years in labour camp and three years in exile, Nijole was first held for seven days in a damp underground cell. Here she caught a severe chill and developed a cough. Eventually, fevered and sick, she endured the twenty-eight day train journey from Vilnius to Mordovia in Russia. She was transported with hardened criminals locked in iron cages, in a cell swarming with bedbugs, and fed just salt fish, bread and water.

As soon as she arrived at the camp, Nijole's health failed, and she was in and out of hospital. Apparently doctors, nurses and fellow-patients fell victim to Nijole's charm and concern for others. Nijole had been brought up a devout Catholic. Even from her earliest years she'd shown immense compassion for the sick, and had done much skilled practical nursing. The saying 'Once a nurse, always a nurse' certainly applies to Nijole: we learn that she was especially caring towards older sick prisoners.

However, the camp labour regime intruded even on convalescence. Nijole still had to complete her 'prisoner's quota' of seventy pairs of gloves per day. Workshop shifts were worked from 6 a.m. to 10 p.m. in an atmosphere thick with industrial dust.

For the whole of this time Nijole received no letters from her relatives in the USA and not one of over 300 letters from Britain. But she was told that they had arrived – and been sent back!

Despatched into exile Nijole was employed first as a cleaner, then as a hospital orderly. Typically she got on well with everybody and rejoiced in the beauty of the Angara river and landscape. In one of her letters she writes: 'Thank God, love and goodness are alive even here in Siberia!'

Now forty-four, Nijole lives with her brother Jonas in Vilnius, where she is attached to a church. Suspected by the KGB of being a 'secret nun', she is officially treated as 'persona non grata,' which in Soviet terms means that she is denied all mail and parcels from abroad. She is also banned from employment as a nurse. But then it's small wonder that the Soviet authorities attempt to contain Nijole Sadunaite – a woman who just by being herself is a potent witness to a life lived joyfully for God.

« Where Does Suffering Come From? »

Human actions differ from those of animals, because they are born out of thought and not carried out purely instinctively. It must be known in advance what a man can and cannot do, what measures help him in his suffering and how to behave during suffering. Without this knowledge all good intentions can come to nothing.

Suffering is essentially linked to evil. It cannot be separated from evil.

What is evil? It is not something positive. It is negative, a deficiency of good. Thomas Aquinas says evil is a loss of something which is necessary to the nature of certain beings: a loss of something which we once possessed, but have no longer (like a lost wing for a bird). Evil is a deficiency, says Augustine. Suffering is also a deficiency; a deficiency of goodness.

Where does suffering come from? Not from God but from the sins of mankind. God is Eternal Love, Eternal Goodness, and could not create suffering. Being unable to understand suffering, people may think that it was created by the Creative Power.

What then is the origin of suffering? The tragedy of paradise lost – the bliss of our first parents with no suffering, no death; and then their sin followed by troubles, tears and death. The loss of supernatural and natural gifts. Hardly had the sin been committed than the storms of passion and suffering spread throughout the world and entered into fierce conflict with mankind, never leaving him.

This is the source of suffering. It comes from a free will which has deviated from the will of God . . .

How good it is to come up constantly against the will of our good Father; to say 'Thy will be done', not only in joy but particularly in suffering. It is then that we come to resemble Christ the Crucified. Frequently and undeservedly I feel so much spiritual joy that it seems my heart will not be able to bear it. And sometimes I feel that if that pure joy could be shared out among all the sons and daughters of this earth they would all be joyful, and no suffering or pain would be left.

I want so much to love the good God with burning, fiery zeal. I want to suffer for him so that I can show my gratitude for his love . . .

He is our Father and this tells us so much! How fortunate we are.

If only everyone could recognize and love that good God, the Father of us all, then there would truly be heaven on earth.

« Nijole's Parable of Suffering »

Two people were sitting in prison for embezzlement. A good friend of theirs who knew about their misfortune threw two bags of money to them through the window of their cell so they could pay back the embezzled money and obtain their release. The money bags happened to strike the men's foreheads as they were thrown in. One of them, angered by this, didn't even bother to look in his bag but threw it straight back out of the window. The other was able to restrain himself: he looked in the bag and was then only too happy to put up with the pain it had caused. This gift not only helped to get him out of prison but also to live without cares for the rest of his life.

Suffering is like that bag of money. It is not properly recognized. When it is thrown at us through a window, we run away from it. Only by recognizing it can we use it or want to use it. Anyone who looks on suffering as his greatest enemy will never learn to suffer as befits a child of God.

« Nijole And Nadia »

(Nijole Sadunaite remembers the friends who shared her fate and whom she left behind in labour camp, and in particular Nadia Usoyeva.)

Nadia Usoyeva is a girl of remarkable goodness and tact. She is a very decent and high-minded Russian Orthodox. We were like sisters, only unfortunately she was hardly ever permitted to 'take a vacation' at the labour camp. It's a real miracle where that fragile girl gets her strength! Five years of punishment cell and strict-regime prison with hardly a break – starvation, cold and ridicule. She is a true heroine; we should kneel to her!

Quiet, calm, always smiling, with a prayer on her lips. I never heard her utter an impatient or rough word. She goes to the punishment cell smiling and returns smiling. Exhausted, blue with cold, she looks terrible, but she smiles – not only at us but at her tormenters as well! Her example moved and still moves me to tears. Please write to her yourselves occasionally. She will then be at least partially rewarded for the constant brutality and ridicule she endures. Lord, how much suffering and injustice in this valley of tears!

ANASTAZAS JANULIS

Anastazas Janulis has just served a three-and-a-half-year sentence in a strict-regime labour camp in Mordovia. Now well over sixty, he also served sentences in labour camps from 1947 to 1956.

Believed to be a Jesuit, he has travelled widely among Catholics in Soviet Central Asia. He was arrested in 1980 after typewriters, a duplicating machine and *samizdat* literature were found in his home. At his trial he was charged with 'slander against the Soviet system'. His relatives were not told of the date of his trial, and it was only after long argument that one of two of them were allowed into the courtroom.

Despite injustice and hardship in the labour camp, his letter to a young schoolgirl is full of optimism and joy in his surroundings. There is little doubt that however hard the physical deprivation, such an experience brings to some a heightened perception. Many passages in this letter have an almost lyrical quality, and bear the hallmark of a mind attuned to God through his creation – even of the smallest sparrow.

It is a far cry from his previous intellectual activity in publishing to the humble task of glove-making. Yet Anastazas holds all things in proportion. He thanks God for prison work and looks forward to meeting his Maker, wearing a pair of gloves he has made himself in the prison workshop!

At his trial Anastazas Janulis made a bold final speech: he emphasized that, as only atheists were allowed freedom of the press, Christians were forced to use underground publishing methods. He summed up by quoting Ignatius Loyola's famous prayer.

It takes a courageous Christian to make such utterances in the very teeth of the atheist judiciary in its own court.

'Teach us good Lord, to serve thee as thou deservest; to give and not to count the cost; to fight and not to heed the wounds; to toil and not to seek for rest; to labour and not to ask for any reward, save that of knowing that we do thy will.'

Ignatius Loyola

« Letter to a Schoolgirl »

What can I write about myself? Both a great deal and nothing. In my thoughts I write many letters to you. Unfortunately they do not reach their destination, for those thoughts are not set down on paper. And what is set down loses the colour of my daily existence.

The cross I wear on my breast bears the inscription, 'I am nailed to the cross of Christ'. Oh how I wish for these words to come true in me, to be worthy of them. It is written, God loves the cheerful giver. That is why I sing Te Deum in my soul, because God has chosen me for sacrifice to follow his Son's path, if necessary, from the Garden of Gethsemane to Golgotha. Of course, I miss the altar and the organ. Now my church is the shrine of nature. Nature is the Creator's open book, substituting for the gospel. While reading this book, it is very easy to pray, not only in brief celebrations, but also by practising mental prayer.

Many doves fly into our yard. Seeing them I remember Christ's words, 'Be harmless as doves,' or my mother's words, 'May God bestow the Holy Spirit upon you!' The dove is a symbol of the Holy Spirit. Seeing an ordinary grey sparrow on the roof, I seem to hear Christ's words: 'You are of more value than many sparrows', and not one of them falls without the knowledge of the heavenly Father . . . Seeing the poorest little flower, I remember Christ's parable: 'Isn't life worth more than food? And isn't the body worth more than clothes? Look at the birds . . . Look how the wild flowers grow . . . not even King Solomon with all his wealth had clothes as beautiful . . .'

I worship the Creator, for really I now have nothing to worry about. Providence provides for everything through its creatures. I am fed and clothed and rested. One need only love God and everything will be for the good. Even work will become a blessing!

Prayer and work are two wings on which I rise towards heaven. When God someday calls me to himself, I will not go to him with bare hands, but wearing gloves: the gloves I made with my own hands.

All five senses given man help to remind us of God and unite with him in mental prayer. Living here it is of the utmost importance to live with God and for God. The man who lives with God becomes convinced that everything is relative: happiness and unhappiness, joy and suffering, even freedom and captivity, health and illness.

At present, I am healthy. I take no notice of minor ailments. The climate here is extreme. The wind changes often: it blows from the south, then suddenly it's from the west or east. It's dry, there was practically no rain this year. It is hot, stifling. Now the weather is gradually getting colder: the nights are very mild. I had a good opportunity to enjoy them. I had the good luck to spend several nights outdoors. Lord, what a blessing! You lie with your eyes open and see the miraculous beauty of the universe. Watching the stars and the sky I remember the words of the great Spaniard: 'How wretched seems the earth when you look at the starry sky . . .' How much could be written about the night! It is with good reason that poets sing its praises. I spent much time in prayer and reflection on those nights.

Where did I not travel on those nights! I borrowed the Great Bear from the sky, harnessed it with the stars and . . . set out across the sleeping world . . . Flying over the fields, forests and lakes of my sleeping homeland I seemed to hear the words of Maironis: 'The world is asleep . . . But many hearts are awake.' Who are they? They are the restless hearts. A mother is keeping watch over her child's cradle; a priest is awake, not having finished his breviary because of various duties during the day.

Unfortunately, there are also others who are keeping watch.

JULIUS SASNAUSKAS

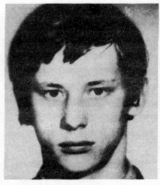

In a list of prisoners and their photographs published last year, one very young face demands a second look. Unsmiling, bewildered, the face of Julius Sasnauskas looks out at us. A young Lithuanian Catholic, Julius was only twenty when he was arrested after a house-search at his home in Vilnius. His mother, Dalia, waits anxiously at home for his return. It will be a long wait, for her son was sentenced to a year and a half's strict-regime labour camp, followed by five years' exile in Russia.

The KGB have long memories. When Julius Sasnauskas refused to give evidence against Viktoras Petkus he was expelled from school with three other boys. All four were then conscripted into the army and sent t a distant part of the USSR. In poor health previously, Julius was found to have severe spinal defects and was discharged from military service, only to be arrested almost at once for possessing *samizdat* publications and being involved with a nationalist group.

Despite worsening health he was sentenced and sent off to a strict-regime camp.

Friends and acquaintances were outraged and many signed a petition to President Brezhnev demanding the young prisoner's release. In their appeal they stated: 'Everyone acquainted with Julius Sasnauskas knows him to be a young man of rare decency and moral standing.'

It was no use. Like most petitions it was ignored, even though Julius' health deteriorated and he developed an inflammatory bone condition.

Now he is serving his term of exile. In his youth he shows an older man's wisdom; as a member of this young generation he shows a touching concern for the next.

In an extract from a letter home he describes prison conditions in Tomsk before his journey into exile.

'In Tomsk I was again put into prison. More searches and a long wait before the cell doors opened for me. The cell was small . . . there were no fewer than ten of us in it. A cement floor, two-tier wooden bunks, the window nailed up so as to be barely visible. Hot and suffocating. In the middle of the night legions of bugs emerge. I spent only one night in this prison; on Friday after the midday meal, I was moved off in a convoy bound for Parabel . . . I now live in a hostel on the edge of town. I cannot travel the least distance without the local commandant's permission. I am to be employed as a fitter and sanitary technician.'

Marked down so early by the authorities for punishment, how many more times during his lifetime will Julius Sasnauskas find himself in exile?

« Sow in Fertile Soil »

At a decisive moment of life, when we must witness to our human worth and the strength of our ideals, how important it is to understand the need for sacrifice. In the presence of those great virtues which we are called on to protect and defend, personal losses pale.

I simply pay tribute to that miraculous religion which unites men's minds and hearts and is an inexhaustible source of love. May the Lord open the eyes of all who have not found their way to it.

We can lose our homeland, our freedom, the warmth of home and friends, but so long as our spirit remains alive, we shall find those values within us. All-creative faith will produce this. If in all the cross-currents we manage to maintain our youthful ideals, not even the worst hardships, losses and failures will be able to defeat us. The defence of great ideals demands constant struggle and sacrifice. Faithfulness is demonstrated not by a short-lived enthusiasm, but by a whole life, even at the cost of life itself. There can be no abstract love for either God or homeland; there is only the love whose existence in our hearts we prove by our actions.

Celebrated deeds and anonymous patient daily work both have equal value when inspired by the love of Christ . . . But what if we don't see, perhaps will never see, the fulfilment of our hopes? Even the farmer, as he sows his seed in the ground, does not see the end result of his work. But harvest time will come and the seed sown in tears will turn to joy, although perhaps it will be others who gather the fruits of the harvest. For centuries our soil has been known for its fertility, and once the years of frost and drought pass, it will again yield bountiful harvests. Let us therefore sow the seed with a bold hand.

If more and more young people today want to prove their fidelity to God and country, let them learn and work: patiently responsibly, lovingly. All this demands no less sacrifice than imprisonment . . .

Parabel has few native inhabitants, mostly strangers seeking their fortune. People are engrossed in their own troubles.

Their existence is not easy and consolation is sought only in alcohol.

'Well what does the Russian Ivan need?' they say of themselves. 'Bread and alcohol, nothing else!'

. . . Can we discover true values and be truly happy without ever experiencing suffering, hardship, or loss?

'Through hope to the stars, through the cross to light,' the old saying goes. And that is a tried and tested truth. Transformed, meaningful pain is a prime means of growth. Like a bolt of lightning, it sheds light on the depths of the soul, it jolts and refreshes. A calm, trouble-free life amounts to vegetation. Even in nature, the sky is clearest after a storm.

Unfortunately, we cannot always see the purpose and meaning of events and, as the time of trial approaches, we hide in fear. That is self-deception. Only by experiencing pain and giving it meaning can man renew himself, and reach the spiritual heights.

We live at a critical time. We must stop to reflect: Where are we going? What will we bequeath to future generations?

VLADAS LAPIENIS

If you are only allowed to write two letters every month, you weigh your words carefully.

When Vladas Lapienis wrote his Easter letter from labour camp he discussed hardship and fortitude. No doubt he wrote from experience; he was serving a five-year sentence. Three years in a strict-regime camp, followed by two years' exile in Siberia.

Vladas Lapienis is a Lithuanian Catholic and was arrested in Vilnius in October 1976. He had been distributing copies of the *Chronicle of the Lithuanian Catholic Church* and was charged with 'disseminating slanderous literature'. At his trial he looked pale and ill and his voice was so weak that he could hardly be heard. However, he managed to get a copy of his final statement to a friend who published it in a subsequent issue of the *Chronicle*. In it he declares passionately that he feels no guilt, that under the International Declaration of Human Rights he has a right to speak the truth and defend his religion. Despite all efforts by the KGB to suppress it the *Chronicle* continues to publish; such statements as Vladas' are circulated and eventually reach the West.

Vladas Lapienis is not a young man. He was born in 1906. A pensioner with a heart complaint must find life difficult enough. But in a strict-regime camp, then in exile in Siberia – this must involve hardship too awful to contemplate. Alongside the enforced labour and bitter cold, Vladas must have felt great isolation. Not only was he far from his homeland but his mail was not passed onto him. The authorities in labour camps often insist that all letters received by prisoners must be written in Russian, otherwise they are confiscated. Lithuanian is not acceptable.

Despite such privation, Vladas' own letter is full of joy. Where some might despair, he sees his sentence as an opportunity to grow in faith. What can the camp censor have made of such positive Christian affirmation?

« An Easter Letter »

One who can sacrifice everything for love – happiness, freedom, health, even life – is truly a lover.

That is how Christ loved people.

Thomas à Kempis said that not a single hour of Christ's earthly life was without pain. But are we not trying to find a way out of suffering? Are we not trying to take any other road than the one our Redeemer followed?

If by chance we do put on a martyr's crown then, according to the apostle James, we should count it a real joy to have experienced all kinds of tests. Let us understand that the testing of our faith makes for fortitude. We mature in strength through works in order that we may become perfect and strong.

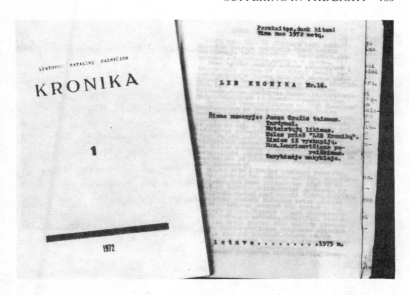

Two issues of 'Chronicle of the Lithuanian Catholic Church', including the first, from 1972. This clandestine journal reports the activities of Lithuanian Catholics.

It is said that we must patiently bear all hardships because this gains us great joy in heaven. But even here on earth, hardships become light for a Christian who truly loves Jesus and carries his cross with him.

Only we who carry our cross with Jesus experience a happiness the world cannot know. We are on the hill called Calvary, but we are already celebrating victory in heaven.

As James wrote, 'My brothers, consider yourselves fortunate when all kinds of trials come your way, for you know when your faith succeeds in facing such trials the result is the ability to endure. Make sure that your endurance carries you all the way without failing, so that you may be perfect and complete, lacking nothing.'

RUDOLF KLASSEN

'I have never celebrated Christmas as I did this year.'

Rudolf Klassen wrote these words in a letter from prison

The members of the Council of Prisoners' Relatives have to travel many hundreds of miles to meet. They aim to support prisoners' families and to make their plight known.

camp on New Year's Eve 1981. But they were not words of self-pity or complaint. They were written in a mood of wonder at the spiritual freedom experienced in captivity.

Rudolf Klassen is a fifty-two-year-old Baptist from Karaganda in Kazakhstan. As a member of an unregistered Baptist church he was kept under regular surveillance by the authorities. His home was frequently searched for literature printed on the clandestine 'Christian' printing presses, and several of his friends were arrested as a result of such searches.

Klassen himself was arrested – for a second time – in June 1980, and sentenced to three years' labour camp for his involvement in Christian youth work.

At the beginning of June 1983, just seventeen days before his release, he was transferred from labour camp to an investigation prison.

During interrogation Klassen was forced to stand for hours against a wall with his hands raised while he was repeatedly beaten. He was then warned that he would receive even harsher treatment if he so much as glanced at the people in the courtroom during his trial. Sadly, because of this stricture, he was unable to see that his wife Talita and four other Christians were sitting anxiously on the public benches in the court.

It was only during a brief visit to her husband after his trial that Talita learned the reason for his refusal to look at her. She reports he was very close to breaking-point but refused to renounce his faith or his work in the unregistered church in exchange for freedom.

In the following letter Rudolf Klassen reveals the great comfort derived from the many messages and cards he received at Christmastime.

'Once strangers, we are now friends, brought together by the blood of Christ.' In these words we see true unity in action. For while free Christians write letters to those in captivity and pray for them, there is little doubt that those behind bars pray for their fellow-Christians too. Such reciprocal support demonstrates the love and concern of Christians world-wide.

'Nothing can replace personal spiritual contact by way of correspondence and greetings cards on Christian holidays from friends . . . What a joy that would bring them!' (*From the letter written in 1975 by Fr Gleb Yakunin and Lev Regelson to the World Council of Churches.*)

« No Christmas Like It »

I wanted to sit down earlier today to write a letter, but there were all kinds of interruptions until this evening. First tidying up, then the superintendent brought in a fir tree, and we had to put it up in the 'Red Corner' and decorate it for the New Year. Now they have set up a record-player for us and loud music is playing. I can't help thinking of Moses and Pharaoh's magicians. Moses threw down his staff and it turned into a snake. The magicians did the same, but the difference was that Moses' snake swallowed theirs up.

Today I have a very difficult task, which I simply don't know how to deal with. You see, in the past sixteen days I have received 110 letters and cards; this is the love of Christ in action. How can I answer them all in one letter? To all of you from the bottom of my heart I say 'Thank you so much!'

I don't complain at my fate; no, I thank the Lord for this path. There is a saying: 'You won't know happiness until you have experienced the bitterness of misfortune.' And I must say that I've had to taste this in order to see happiness as a blessing from God.

The Lord spoke of John the Baptist as a lamp burning and giving light. I would like to apply these words to you, my dear friends. I have never celebrated Christmas as I did this year. And although I was in confined circumstances my spiritual freedom was broad.

I remember I once heard of a Christian prisoner who drew a cross, and above it he wrote 'height', below 'depth' and on each side 'length' and 'breadth'; on the cross he wrote 'love'. It makes sense. Vorkuta, Tashkent, Belorussia, Siberia – the cross of Christ unites us, and not just in some vague way, for we experience bliss. Today we can say to our foes as Joseph did to his brothers: 'You intended to do me harm, but the Lord has brought good out of it.' Glory to God! . . .

On Christmas Day, 25 December, I received twenty-five greetings . . . What can I say about all these messages? It's impossible to write it all down. I'll say just one thing: 'Once strangers, we are now friends, brought together by the blood of Christ.' These messages brought me warmth, light, encouragement, joy and comfort. May God bless you all abundantly; this will be my constant prayer to God.

CARDINAL WYSZYNSKI

While many in Poland referred to Cardinal Wyszynski as the 'uncrowned King of Poland', others dubbed him 'the Iron Cardinal'.

When we read his many sermons, addresses and letters it is easy to see why he might have earned such a name. In confronting evil Cardinal Wyszynski chose to make firm demands from a position of power – a spiritual and moral power inspired by God.

His sermons are inspiring; sometimes didactic. His letters to the authorities, his administrative papers are closely reasoned, weighty documents.

And yet – he writes for his people as a true shepherd of souls. Brought up in the deep but simple faith of the peasantry, steeped in fable and folklore, perhaps Cardinal Wyszynski betrays his real self in the moving account of a prisoner's Christmas. Stripped of all the trappings of office, the priest Cardinal Wyszynski ministers to his little flock and finds 'serene joy', much as the earliest Christians might have experienced it.

In the retelling of the fable of the crow and the pine tree, printed in the last section, he uses his knowledge of folklore as a powerful teaching tool. 'Premonitions of Spring' has a simple, almost lyrical quality.

These pieces demonstrate the Cardinal's immense versatility and his extraordinary sensitivity to both the intellectual abilities and the spiritual needs of different people. Truly he was what he longed to be: a shepherd and bishop of souls.

« Christmas in Prison »

Christmas Eve has the same character as last year. Nevertheless, we have received a small pine tree which we decorate with what is to hand, and the dinner menu is closer to tradition. The house is silent. We give some unleavened bread to the housekeeper's assistant but we don't dare to attack the ideology of the guards. Lack of generosity? Perhaps. I don't think they would appreciate our gesture. They are serious and morose. But here on the first floor, we are full of serene joy.

After 11 p.m. we start singing matins in our chapel. Sister is following it with the text in her hands. After midnight I celebrate the first sung mass, followed by two others. My flock sing Christmas carols. We are quite happy in our little chapel, without flowers, with ordinary candles which smoke continually, in front of Christ who has chosen to be with us today. We have decided to spend the Christmas festival together. Nobody must feel alone. We are making efforts to overcome each other's nostalgia – all symptoms of this are a defeat. God, who has sent us this trial, wants us to help each other. We pray that our families should not be sad. We put off our work until later: during the next two days we are not going to touch books or pens. Now we can say anything to each other without restraint, even silly things. Absolute liberty for the children of God.

We continue singing until two in the morning. We pray for the church, the pope and the bishops, for our families in the church and for our relatives. We feel that prayer has created in us a spiritual state which is satisfying to our Lord. Our last prayer is for our guards and for the soldiers mounting guard outside, in the snowy forest. They are the unhappiest among us – we know this full well.

At 2.30, our floor is all in darkness. Serene dreams. We are confident that God does not regret having kept us in prison for this festival when the 'Key of David' was brought into the world.

PART SEVEN

LIGHT ACROSS
THE BARRIERS

The international church

DMITRI DUDKO

There is something particularly selfless and moving about Father Dmitri Dudko's letter to Italian Catholics. Here is an Orthodox priest, a man who has suffered physical, mental and spiritual humiliation for his faith. Yet he steps outside his own traumas and his church's persecution.

Christian love is the heart of true Russian Orthodoxy. In the following letter Father Dmitri demonstrates that love in his deep concern for the spiritual prognosis of Italian Catholics. He pleads for their support and for urgent ecumenical activity before it is too late. At the same time the sense of the mission of the Russian Orthodox church to the rest of the world is apparent in every word he writes to his 'brothers in Christ'.

The Soviet authorities know well that Father Dmitri's influence and fame have spread to the West, particularly among young people. In this letter to Italian Catholics he mentions the car accident in which he broke both legs. This accident occurred in 1975 when he was under increasingly harsh pressure for his religious activities. A lorry reversed into a car in which Fr Dmitri was a passenger. The lorry driver immediately drove off without waiting to see what had happened. The police refused to investigate the incident and no legal proceedings were instituted. Friends of Father Dmitri are convinced that the whole incident was engineered by the KGB – it effectively put him out of action for some time. Their efforts were counter-productive, however, for once Fr Dmitri recovered, young supporters never left his side for fear of further 'accidents'.

When news of Father Dmitri's injuries reached the West he drew sympathy and prayerful support from many Christians, including Italian Catholics.

Such Christian empathy, transcending national and denominational boundaries, goes beyond mere sympathy. It bodes well for Christian renewal and solidarity in both East and West, and furthers the cause so dear to Father Dmitri – unity.

« Separated Too Long »

Dear Italian Catholics, brothers in Christ!

I was overjoyed to hear that you are trying to help us Orthodox Christians living in Russia. I hear you are even trying to learn Russian!

May Christ save you! He is our help on Golgotha here in Russia, but he is not just our help, he is able to help your brothers living in Italy or anywhere else, and those who have not yet been born. For our disease is threatening you too.

Atheism is a plague which attacks the whole human organism. If we can stop this plague spreading we will not just stop the spread of a disease but will come that much closer to eternity.

I have already experienced the effects of your fellow-feeling several times in my life. Right after the car accident, when I was lying in bed with both legs broken, I received a number of sympathetic letters. I could feel the heartbeat of these letters and my own blood began to course more quickly in my veins. Your letters gave me new strength and summoned me to action with their expressions of solidarity.

Yes, we must stand in solidarity against the onslaught of our common enemy. He is trying to bring us all, everything, to destruction.

We have been separated too long: this must stop now! It is rather paradoxical: when our enemy wasn't so terrible, perhaps separation was necessary so that we could understand ourselves better, and gather our strength in the calmness of our own confession. But now, when the enemy is in his final fury, separation can be just a form of egoism. Our times demand ecumenism. We must seize the opportunity for unity so that we can learn to help each other as we ought.

Any undertaking has its shortcomings, and so does the contemporary ecumenical movement, when we just meet at conferences, hear official speeches, sit down to banquets. Ecumenism must penetrate deeper, to the heart of suffering modern man. It must listen to his heart beating; and then it must not be ashamed to bow right down to man's chapped and dusty feet, just as Christ knelt to wash the feet of his disciples. Our feet must walk in the right path. This is the path of love. Ecumenism is love for one another. Ecumenism without love is just 'sounding brass, or a tinkling cymbal'.

YOUNG SLOVAKS

A letter written by young people for young people, this appeal sent by young Slovaks to their fellow-Catholics is proof that the state has not stifled the Catholic church in Czechoslovakia.

The extract featured here is headed 'Hope', but every line betrays impatience, passion, fervour, youthful enthusiasm.

In an earlier paragraph the young authors courageously announce, 'The Party has sentenced the church to death.' It is evident to anyone who reads this letter that the church refuses to die.

It is a strange fact that although the majority of the people of Czechoslovakia are Catholics, the Catholic church there has historically been rather weak. In the Czech part of the Republic, hopes of national rebirth have traditionally been inspired by Protestant ideas; and in Slovakia the Catholic church became tragically implicated in collaborating with Hitler. After the Communists came to power in 1948 they found in the Catholic church a weakened victim which they were able to attack with great success. During the 1950s thousands of priests and bishops, monks and nuns, and Catholic intellectuals, teachers and writers were imprisoned and exiled.

Today the official Catholic church in Czechoslovakia is in a straitjacket, its clergy merely paid cyphers of the state. It has been said of Czechoslovakia that the state pays its priests to neglect their ministry. Certainly some clergy are exploited, used as mere puppets or mouthpieces for state propaganda. All clergy are expected to join the official government-backed *Pacem in Terris* movement. This is a movement dedicated to promoting 'peace on earth' – surely something Christians would applaud. But it does this by enthusiastically backing all Soviet policies and blaming the West for the dangerous arms race. Meanwhile, Catholic clergy and laypeople who want to preach and live the gospel without interference from the state find themselves under continual pressure.

Pope John Paul II, aware that the *Pacem in Terris* movement was really an attempt to use the church for political ends, opposed it by issuing a decree in March 1982 forbidding all Catholic clergy to indulge in political activity of any kind.

At the same time, however, persecution has refined the church's spiritual life. There are priests and many young people who further the faith through a lively underground church. It is in this church that real mission is accomplished – not in the official church where a servile status quo operates.

There are also signs that certain elderly members of the church hierarchy are emerging from their self-imposed censorship and submissive attitudes. Braver voices are being heard; dissent quietly encouraged.

The young authors of this letter make a positive approach to problems experienced by young and not-so-young believers. There is no evasion of personal responsibilities – no shifting of all blame to the state. Instead we hear a clarion call to young Slovak Catholics for immediate action to ensure a future for the church.

With young Christians like this the church must surely have hope – and a future.

« We Won't Wait! »

Old people, who can remember the days when the church was free, simply hope for the return of better times. They say persecution will eventually cease. Until then they are content to preserve faith, even if only among a small band of believers – in short, mere survival.

But the persecution we are undergoing is quite different from that in the past; and we don't know how long it will last. Maybe pressure is easing, but a long time could pass before Christians are granted equality.

We young people know only our present conditions. We are not content to wait patiently for better times. We place no hope in political change. We seek rather to follow Christ here and now, so that even in a hostile environment we may fulfil our Christian mission: to be the light of the world. If we can manage this, we will become a source of hope for many.

As Christians, we don't feel as if we're on a sinking ship. The 'religious crisis' here, and throughout the world, doesn't cloud our vision – we know that Christianity will emerge from such a crisis renewed and purified . . .

We don't think Christianity is declining or old-fashioned. We are convinced that it has a message for today's world – that only in Christ does the world have a future. He is the way – nothing else will do.

Although we're still looking for a role in this un-Christian world, we don't yet understand what that role might be. But we know that a treasure intended for all mankind has been entrusted to us. We know that the world needs us and is waiting for the gospel . . .

Our future is in those who are trying to base their lives on that gospel. They are living proof that Christianity does not demand the impossible . . . Such witness is particularly important nowadays. The church here may have been silenced but there is a growing hunger for spiritual values. The Communist Party has nothing to offer but an improvement in the standard of living. Atheism offers no guidelines on how to live one's life – and practical materialism is no longer sufficient for many people.

The spiritual hunger is confirmed by the many conversions of people who have grown up in the atheist families. It is also evident in the number of full churches. Despite intimidation and harassment, there are churches filled with young people – even in the towns. This is a common phenomenon. Well! What kind of persecution can that be?

The real pressure is applied to the most vulnerable and least visible parts of the church. There aren't enough churches – especially in new housing estates. There is a shortage of priests, and their preaching is monitored. On the other hand, *no one* goes to church in a town nowadays just out of habit, or to please their neighbours or grand-mothers! They go because they want to go, they need to go. By doing so we put our careers at risk, but we cannot give up meeting Christ in the holy communion, or in the fellowship of the church.

In spite of full churches and dedicated priests the church has few opportunities to help the spiritual growth of its members. It also has little chance of responding to those still struggling to find faith. So laymen have to help the priest as much as possible . . .

It isn't easy to be a Christian among unbelievers – to stand out, to be different from others. And so it is vital that we meet and encourage each other. Isolation will destroy us. Attend-ance at church is not enough – one can remain just as isolated there. We have discovered that we need to learn and pray together, to discuss our faith, grow spiritually, and solve our practical problems in a Christian spirit.

We have found ways to do this. An ordinary occasion like spending a holiday with a friend who shares our beliefs is important. This does not mean that we have a right to be exclusive, to adopt a 'holier than thou' attitude. The gift which we have received *must* be shared to serve the whole church and human family.

Perhaps these things are taken for granted in other parts of the world. For us, they prove that the church here in Slovakia is alive. It is not dying. It has a future.

Our future lies with young people who have a scientific yet Christian point of view. It lies in young Christian families who share their spiritual life and raise children prepared to face today's world.

Our future lies in small communities of believers – people of similar age and interests, who by trying to live their faith fully become an example and help to those around them. Our hope is that Christianity will continue to enrich our culture. Perhaps every new Christian song written is a significant sign of Christian vitality . . .

Our future lies in Christian movements – well-known or not. Our hope is in solidarity and friendship with believers in other countries . . . Our future is also in coming together with different Christian denominations – ecumenism, as yet in its infancy here, yet growing up from grassroots level through personal contacts . . .

Our hope too is in our Pope, who well knows our situation here in Slovakia. Our hope is founded on unity with the whole church, itself founded on the Rock, against which the gates of hell cannot prevail.

CHRISTIAN SEMINAR

'We want the world!' declared Vladimir Poresh at his trial. Other active members of the Moscow Christian Seminar felt the same pressing need to unite with Christians both inside and outside the Soviet Union. They made a small but significant start by appealing to young Italian Catholics. The Seminar considered it one of their prime aims to contact young Christians of other major confessions for a free exchange of views.

There is little doubt that there are many similar groups of young Christians in Russia who feel deeply that their only hope is to unite with young believers across national and denominational boundaries. They reach out for such ecumenical co-operation and long to find strength through such support.

Traditionally, 'Holy Russia' saw herself as having a special mission to other faiths, and to help a fallen world to unite in Christ's love. The idea is still cherished by many Russian Orthodox Christians today.

The Soviet authorities saw the Seminar's appeal to Christians of other nationalities as a political threat – a mistaken view, for the Seminar's aims were entirely non-political.

ХРИСТИАНСКИЙ   СЕМИНАР
ПО ПРОБЛЕМАМ   РЕЛИГИОЗНОГО
ВОЗРОЖДЕНИЯ   МОСКВА.

ОРГАНИЗАЦИЯ   МОЛОДЫХ
ИТАЛЬЯНСКИХ   КАТОЛИКОВ
"СОБОРНОСТЬ И ОСВОБОЖДЕНИЕ"

Обращение по поводу репрессий
против основателей Семинара
Александра Огородникова и Владимира Пореша.

Дорогие друзья!

Многое говорит за то, что именно наше поколение, т.е. мы с вами, призваны к великому творческому усилию – преодолению тысячелетней расколотости Церкви, а с нею – всего христианского мира. Россия стала христианским народом тогда, когда назревало это разделение и, быть может, для того, чтобы это разделение предотвратить. Но Россия была еще слишком незрела, чтобы свое призвание осознать, а Рим и Византия слишком заняты своими проблемами, чтобы бескорыстным духовным взором, с высоты своей мудрости вглядеться в глубоко самобытную и в то же время вселенски-отзывчивую душу нового великого народа, пришедшего ко Христу.

Много исторических бед выросло из этого непонимания, и на наши с вами плечи ложится труд это отчуждение преодолеть. Мы осознаем себя представителями молодой России, России будущего, и в то же время чувствуем, что питаемся из самых глубинных корней изначальной русской духовности. Поэтому, рассказывая вам о России, мы рассказываем вам о себе, в надежде, что вы ответите нам тем же – откроете себя нам.

Наш поэт сказал:

Умом Россию не понять,
Аршином общим не измерить,
У ней особенная стать –
В Россию можно только верить...

Он был прав, но мы хотим дополнить его мысль: Россию не понять умом, как нельзя умом понять Евангелие, нельзя измерить ее, как нельзя меркой закона оценить Нагорную проповедь, в нее можно только верить, в том же смысле, как мы веруем в Церковь. Ибо то, что мы знаем, не является предметом веры, а мы исповедуем именно веру в единую, кафолическую святую, соборную и апостольскую Церковь.

Суть России – как мы ее понимаем – в том, что она изначально захотела стать Христовым народом, Святой Русью; в том, что она захотела построить по Евангелию, и только по Евангелию, всю свою народную, т.е. государственную, социальную, культурную и семейную жизнь. Идея безумная – не более и не менее безумная, чем само Евангелие. Насколько мы поняли из нескольких встреч с представителями вашего братства, вы сейчас не так уж далеки от этого безумного замысла. А ведь вы – это молодая Италия, и, надо надеяться, будущее католичества. Мы хотим, чтобы вы оценили всю серьезность этого духовного факта – Россия приняла эту идею в самое сердце еще тысячу лет назад и все эту тысячу лет, изживая тяжкие беды и соблазны, томилась и трудилась лишь над тем, чтобы это коренное чаяние осуществить в реальности.

В своем евангельском безумии Россия верила и продолжает верить, что искупительный подвиг Христа достаточен, чтобы грех был побежден

The first page of a letter from young Russian Christians to young Italian Catholics. Many in Russia long to see age-old barriers come down.

The first of the following extracts is from a document sent to an Italian organization of young Catholics – 'Communione e Liberazione'.

It was written before the arrest of two of the signatories in late 1979.

In the second, the writers appeal to young Americans to support them in their spiritual development.

Youth appeals to youth in these letters: 'We represent the youth of Russia, the Russia of the future . . . So when we tell you about Russia we are telling you about ourselves, and we hope you will respond to us in the same way, and reveal yourselves to us.

Our poet says:

> Russia cannot be understood by the intellect:
> It cannot be measured by a normal yardstick.
> It has its own peculiar make-up –
> You can only believe in Russia.

« Appeal To Young Catholics »

Dear Friends,

There are many signs that our generation – you as well as us – is called to make a great effort to overcome the thousand-year-old division in the church and the whole of the Christian world . . .

The essence of Russia consists in the desire she has shown from the very beginning to become Christ's nation – Holy Russia. It lies in her desire to build her national life – social, cultural, administrative and family life – according to the gospel alone. The idea is insane, but no less insane than the gospel itself.

As far as we can gather from meetings with members of your brotherhood you are not far off this insane idea yourselves. You are the youth of Italy; and the Catholics of the future. We want you to appreciate the seriousness of this fact. Russia took this idea to its heart a thousand years ago. Throughout those thousand years, through misfortune and temptation, she has struggled for one thing only: to turn into reality her desire to become Christ's nation. . .

A young nation could only have fulfilled this calling with the help of other more experienced and mature nations.

To struggle against sin Russia would have needed the teaching of Christian law; to build a society based on communal love she would have needed wise Roman law; to resist the pagan hordes from Asia she would have needed the help of the Byzantine Empire and the Christian knights of Europe. She would have needed all this . . . so that eventually she might pour out on foreign brothers the lavish flood of Christian freedom which transfigures life on earth. Russia has more than enough of that love for which a weary world is searching.

If this co-operation, this exchange of ecclesiastical and national values, did not take place a thousand years ago, then it must take place now!

It is we who must do this, with your help. We probably don't know the full measure of your achievements, or the value of your gifts, but we are capable of understanding them if you help us. Show us in concrete terms, in action, the full strength of your loyalty to Jesus Christ, and we shall respond with all the love of Christ which lives in us, and teach you Christian freedom. Then together we can begin a creative life in him. For we are convinced that this is Russia's calling, and following Christ we are determined to put this calling into effect . . .

In all her defencelessness this Russia appeals to you, to your freedom, courage and honour, to your justice and compassion, to your consciences as disciples of Christ. Do not allow the pagan savages of our own time to smother in its cradle the baby whose name is Russia – Russia of the future.

Her life, or death, must depend on your faith and resolve. On your love and your trust in this Russia of the future.

Christ wished her to become your child as well. Protect her now, and save her from death. Only then will you be able to love her as she will love you.

Our common future is in your hands. We rely on you, our brothers.

Signed Members of the Christian Seminar on Problems of the Religious Renaissance: Vladimir Burtsev, Viktor Popkov, Tatyana Shchipkova, Lev Regelson, Vladimir Sokolov.

« Young Russia To Young America »

In the spiritual searchings and struggles of contemporary mankind we, and you, have undertaken the most dangerous and thankless task – to be the first reconnaissance brigade in the new world.

The spirituality we have discovered takes us out of the world of necessity and social obligation; it looks to the future. Our time is a time of creation. The energy of the future, which will erupt with new force, is accumulating in our time – a time of painful self-determination and moral purification.

We are all in need of a deeper and warmer type of communication. The force of active love must transfigure our life and the world around us.

The time has come for us, living as we do on different continents and raised in different historical traditions, to open our hearts to each other and unite our efforts in creating, searching . . .

It has become impossible to go on living a lie. To exist aimlessly in a frenzied world, engaged in useless, boring occupations. It's unbearable having to endure pointless wearisome arguments, anonymous socialist culture, artificial emotions in our newspapers and lies, lies, lies! . . .

We were taught: 'Man is a proud word!' Yet our experience has shown otherwise. 'Man' can sound very pathetic – at times positively revolting. We are told: 'Everything in Man's name, everything for Man's well-being.' But our experience convinces us that state practice is based on a different premise: Man is stupid, dull, incapable of managing himself, and needs to be strictly controlled . . .

On the edge of human despair, we heard a saving call – the voice of our fathers, our saints.

We discovered Russia.

Like archaeologists, we found traces of Russian religious history and culture under layers of falsehood and taboos. We glimpsed the mystery of the church at work in Russia, and of Christ at work in the world.

Orthodoxy was revealed to us as a conquering force, and not just a quiet haven for weary souls seeking escape from harsh reality. Neither is Orthodoxy an end in itself: it is where spiritual endeavour can begin, working towards new creation . . .

But do not imagine that we have exchanged a totalitarian Communist ideology for totalitarian ecclesiastical legalism.

No! We have come to the church to discover freedom in Christ and unity in the image of the Holy Trinity . . .

Truth is revealed in love. We learned this from the holy fathers. If you want to understand the origins and goal of our brotherhood, then examine attentively the icon of the Holy Trinity by our great artist Andrei Rublyov . . .

In this divided world we shall strive to produce a community which is 'the unity of the spirit in the bond of peace!' . . .

It is not in isolated self-assertion that we discover the depths of our personality. It is in brotherly love in the image of the Holy Trinity.

Christ said: 'Love one another as I have loved you' . . .

Open your hearts to us, as we are opening our own to you.

'Look on the unity of the Holy Trinity, and overcome the hateful division of this world.' (*Sergi of Radonezh*)

PART EIGHT

LIGHT FOR THE FUTURE

Three rays of hope

DMITRI DUDKO

« Russia on the Cross »

The French writer Francois Mauriac says that if he sees light anywhere, it is coming only from Russia. Why? Simply because Russia is Golgotha, and where the cross is, there too is resurrection.

If we think about it seriously, we'll see that we're now participating in the most interesting process in history. If we compare our religiosity with that of the West, the balance will fall to our side. Why? Simply because Golgotha is here, and not there. Can an abundance of material goods bring about a religious rebirth? They say that the Catholics don't know what to do in order to keep people in church. They have everything: books, churches . . . But the people, if they believe at all, do so only weakly. We have nothing. But if people believe here, they are ready to die for their faith.

On the basis of letters received from the West, it's evident that they've taken notice of the Russian church. Some people are even studying the Russian language, in order to participate at least this way in our cross and our resurrection. Such a situation places a great responsibility on us. Whoever believes here, but does not take up Christ's work with greater zeal, earns greater condemnation than if he were in the West. All of us must now become tireless Christian workers: aflame, courageous, fearing nothing.

I appeal especially to the young. We must now labour on behalf of our unbelieving fathers, so that they – many of whom died with no faith – may be raised to life in Christ. Our lot is to labour on behalf of all generations. These are not just high-sounding words. This is beginning. Perhaps not everyone notices it. But it will continue, and nothing can stop it.

Fr Dmitri Dudko carries the characteristic cross found everywhere in Russian Orthodox churches. It is a powerful symbol for Russian Christians today.

CARDINAL WYSZYNSKI

« Sunday 17 January 1954: A Fable »

A crow is perching at the top of a pine tree. He looks about him with an air of superiority, and gives a caw of victory. This phantom imagines that the pine tree owes everything to him: its life, its beauty, its evergreen foliage, the strength with which it struggles against wind and storm. The crow's vanity simply takes your breath away. He imagines he is this peaceable pine tree's benefactor.

Impassive, the pine tree seems unaware of its aggressive guest. Nothing disturbs its meditation. So many clouds, so many migrating birds have passed over the pine tree. They have all gone by . . .

And you, crow, this isn't the place for you either. You're trying to overcome your uncertainty and cowardice by cawing. But I, the pine tree, with my roots buried in the bosom of the earth, I continue to grow. You, wild wanderer, casting your shadow on my shining top, you're just a plaything of the wind. I'll be patient. One day you'll cease your poor monotonous cawing and you'll disappear. What's the use of cawing? It's I who will stay here, meditating and patiently building my future. I'll never stop growing. You won't succeed either in dazzling me or in hiding me from the sun; you won't divert me from the path of my ascension. The forest existed before you came, and the forest will still be here after you've gone.

Is this a fable? No.

« Tuesday, 19 April 1955: Premonitions of Spring »

Snowstorm all day, interspersed by rays of sunlight.

Whirling and whirling! Darkness over the earth again. The wind-driven snow buries the grass. But the earth has already been warmed by the April sun and is melting the snow. The snow falls in vain in April – the cold season has already passed, and nature is striving towards warmth, light and life. There is wintertime, and there is springtime. Your angry efforts, your evil tenacity will be of no use.

If only you knew how much the earth longs for peace and sunlight! Nothing can upset the march of time, nothing can conquer goodness, nothing can make us abandon the habits ingrained in our hearts . . .

For two millennia now, the 'Sun of Justice' has been illuminating the earth with love. We are captivated: our thoughts, our words, our actions are born out of love. All men are seeking a gesture, a look, a consolation. This aspiration is rooted in our nature.

Snow will melt under the heart's rays, even in April. Warm up the world: the April sun is weak but it will come nevertheless. The sun will grow stronger: so will love. We are moving towards the sun, warmth, goodness. Enough of cold and of hard words. Let us open the gates of the Motherland . . .

'The winter is over; the rains have stopped; in the countryside the flowers are in bloom . . .' says the Song of Solomon.

We will not retreat. Onward to the light!